CHANCER

THE STORY OF AN UNBELIEVABLE MAN

Chancer
The Story of an Unbelievable Man

Alan Rowe

First published 2020
United Kingdom

© Alan Rowe, 2020

The right of Alan Rowe to be identified as the Author
of this work has been asserted in accordance with the
Copyright, Designs and Patents Act 1988.

British Library Cataloguing in Publication Data
A catalogue record for this book is available from the British Library

ISBN: 9781673607888
Imprint: Independently published
Printed in Great Britain

Alan Rowe

Dedication

To my family and friends. I have told some of my stories to them over the years and they have often said I should write a book about my life. I have kept putting it off but at the age of 81 years I felt the time was right and now they will all know the full facts of how my life turned out. I hope you the reader will find my story as interesting as they did.

Introduction

They say opportunity only knocks once and you must be ready to grab that opportunity when it comes. My life seems to have turned that rule upside down. Since I was a teenager back in the 1950s, life has presented me with endless opportunities – if anything, too many opportunities for one person to handle. And whether it was wise or foolish, safe or risky, I grabbed each and every one of them with both hands and lived life to the full.

The result is that I have had more jobs than most people have in a dozen lifetimes. I have swung between driving a bus and winning the jackpot in Las Vegas. I have travelled the world and yet have always come home to my native Southampton. I have waited on tables and I have managed pop groups. I have delivered laundry and owned a successful coach company. I have made and lost more than one fortune and still come up smelling of roses.

But among the opportunities, the good and the bad, I have also had more than my fair share of black moments. I have almost lost count of the number of times I have seen the inside of a hospital ward. Today I'm a walking testimony to the skills of NHS doctors and nurses, but thankful that I am still in one piece and still going.

It's been a real roller-coaster of a life and that's why I wanted to share it with my friends, my family and with you, the reader. I hope you will find something to take away from my lifetime of experiences that are often unbelievable – but always true.

There's an old nursery tale about a bad fairy who turns up at a Christening and curses the new-born child with bad luck. I sometimes wonder if that evil fairy was around when I came into the world because as well as having more jobs than anyone else, and having won my fair share of honours, I've also had more accidents – some of them serious – and more good fortune, too. So here they all are – the good times and the bad.

Alan Rowe
January 2020

Chapter One
1940s - A Southampton Childhood

I was born at a maternity home at the top of Winchester road near the junction with The Avenue, Southampton, on the 21st of February 1938 and called Alan Edward Rowe. It was eight days later that my mum (Eve Minnie) wheeled me in a pram 250 yards down the road to number 412 a rented ground floor flat which was where she and my dad (Albert Edward) lived.

Until I was born mum worked in service and dad worked for Pirelli General at Southampton, later being transferred to their Eastleigh factory where he was making arms for the forces and so was exempted from being called up.

I was very lucky that despite the war, we went away for a week's holiday each year. The first I remember was when I was 3 ½ years old and we went to Gurnard on the Isle of Wight. We stayed in a chalet in a farmer's field with several more chalets. Each morning I would walk with Mum up to the gate with the other holidaymakers and I was allowed to carry a milk jug or pail. We would all wait for the farmer to come along with his horse and cart with a milk churn on it. He would then dip a ladle into the churn and pour the milk into our containers. But I wasn't allowed to carry it back in case I fell.

I cannot remember the next two holidays, at Newquay and Ilfracombe, although I have seen photos of me on the beach, but I do remember going to Torquay when I was 6 ½ years old. I asked Dad what was all the ironwork poking up out of the sea. He explained that if Germany invaded it was to stop the landing craft getting ashore.

I had the usual children's ailments such as mumps, measles, whooping cough, chicken pox, and German measles. But I also had my first taste of hospitals and medicine when I had my tonsils out and later when I caught impetigo and the nurse painted blue stuff over the spots. The doctor said I should eat as many bananas as I could, but this was 1948 and bananas were still on ration and only just starting to come back into the shops again. Mum had a special ration book for them. I went to school one day with one of my precious bananas and all the other children wanted to taste it because they had never seen one in their lives.

I also had an attack of quinsy, where your neck swells up and presses against your windpipe making it hard to breathe or drink. I was in bed for four days. The doctor came in at 11 in the morning to examine me. He told my parents he would be back at 4 in the afternoon and if I was no better would have to go to hospital, where they would have to put a tube in my windpipe so I could breathe. Luckily, the fever broke an hour after he left and I could breathe and drink again. I hadn't eaten for four days and was starving so mum cooked me a huge meal.

As well as catching more than my fair share of childhood illnesses, I was also accident prone from the earliest age. Some people go through life without ever having an accident. Others have a few but I must be the exception as I have had 23 accidents. In some I could have been seriously injured or even killed, but fate and good luck have always been on my side.

My Mum told me that when I was two and a half years old she and Dad took me for a walk with our long-haired Collie. When we stopped to rest, I sat on Mum's lap while she wiped my face with a flannel. She said I gave out a scream. At first she told me not to be such a baby but when she took the flannel away there was a trickle of blood running down under my eyelid. She unfolded the flannel and found there was a needle inside. How it got there she did not know but if the cut had been any higher I could have lost sight in my left eye.

Memories of D-Day

I was an only child but I had a lot of other older boys around me during the war years as none of the kids in our area were evacuated. We used to go to the common to play because at Basset Crossroads they had run tram lines under the trees for the trams to park, in case their depots at Shirley and Portswood were bombed in the night. Here we were free to get up to all sorts of mischief.

This was the period immediately before D-Day and American troops had set up a rest camp on the common which became a magnet for us kids. One day they had a bonfire going and were blowing up balloons and letting them float off into the road so that the trams would run over them and they would go off pop. We all asked for one to take home which they gave us, I ran home to show mum and she took it straight away from me. It was some years later that I found out my "balloon" was a Durex – there were no balloons during the war,

Our house had one indoor shelter with metal cages on three sides, in which I used to sleep and one air raid Anderson shelter outdoors. One night the sirens went off, signalling a raid, and Dad took me into the garden. It was a clear night and we could hear the bombs going off in Southampton town centre and docks. Mum was a very heavy sleeper, so dad left her in bed because we never expected bombs on the outskirts of town. As we looked up at the night sky, we saw a silver shape and Dad said, "That's a doodle bug. When its engine cuts out, it just drops to the ground." No sooner had he said this than the thing stopped and came down about 150 yards down the road next to Buck's Garage with a massive explosion. Mum had slept through the lot. The sirens sounded the all clear and we went back to bed I was excited and couldn't wait to tell mum what had happened that night. We later walked down the road and we could see a large hole where a house had previously been.

It was now just weeks before D-Day and troops were pouring into Southampton and down our road where they parked their tanks and lorries. Mum and dad got friendly with the soldiers billeted near us and two or three times a week ten or so of them would come into our house and we would all sit on the floor and listen to records on dad's HMV gramophone.

Two of the men had only recently been married. They were very young so Mum asked them if their wives would like to come down for the weekend and stay with us. Jimmy came from West Bromwich and Taffy from Cardiff. It was getting towards the end of May and they knew something was up so they got their wives to visit. Perhaps they knew it could be their last. It was hot during May and sometimes we would wake up to find 11 or 12 soldiers sleeping on our front lawn as they couldn't sleep in their transports. Then one morning the road was empty, and we knew the invasion had begun.

Of course, we wondered what had happened to "our" lads. Two months later we had a letter to say Taffy had died on the French beaches and later still a letter to say Jimmy had been killed. Mum kept in touch with the woman from West Bromwich for nearly 55 years until she passed away.

I attended Winchester road congregational church (now Isaac Watts) every Sunday with Mum. Dad came now and again. I joined the Life Boys and later the 13th Southampton Boys' Brigade. At 14, I took the Sunday morning service at the church with two others to help me - a special day. I went to Hollybrook school which was in Winchester road in those days and then to Shirley and then Shirley Warren school.

Keen on Sports

I'd always been keen on sport from a young age and first started to play football for the Life Boys then the Boys Brigade. I then joined the Sunday League, which had just been formed, and played for Basset Rovers and later for The Crown pub. I played for Shirley Warren School in football, cricket and chess, played football for several teams in Southampton Junior League and Senior League, and for Sway in the New Forest League.

In those days, some teams had pitches that were open fields during the week so, before we could play, we had to move the horses and cows off them. And even then you had to watch you didn't step into a cowpat while playing!

Adventures in East Grinstead

When I was nine years old something happened that had a big influence on my life. My parents took me to see my Uncle Bert and Aunty Bess at East Grinstead, in Sussex. Mum had not seen her brother for 11 years and we went by coach and bus over the Easter weekend. I met my cousins Morris, Betty, Jane, Stan and Mary for the first time and played with them all weekend. Mary was only two years older than me and was like a big sister. I had great fun discovering my new family because at home I was an only child and often played on my own.

When it came to the school summer holidays, I told my parents I wanted to go up to East Grinstead again but Mum said, "We can't afford to take you up and come back a couple of weeks later to collect you." But I said, "I can go by myself - I know the way." At first they said no - but I kept on so much that in the end they agreed.

They put me onto a Royal Blue coach to Victoria coach station in London, where I crossed over two main roads to catch the 708 Green Line down to East Grinstead. Luckily, the bus stopped outside my Aunt and Uncle's house in London road.

During one holiday, when I was nine and a half years old I stayed once again at East Grinstead with Uncle Bert and Aunty Bess. He had a wood business and I used to go with my cousins Stan and Morris out to the woods in the lorry and they would cut down the trees and put them on the lorry and we would take them back to the yard, where they had an old hut left by the army. Inside was a big saw which they used to cut the wood up into logs then throw them in a pile. There was a rope hanging down from one of the metal supports that held the hut together and I wanted to be like Tarzan so I got hold of the rope, climbed to the top of the pile of logs and started swinging back and forth. Suddenly the rope slipped down the girder and I went crashing to the ground and landed on an axe that had been left there. I gave a yell and everybody came running. When I pulled down my short trousers there was a large cut on my bum, so Uncle rushed me back to get Aunty's opinion.

We all piled into the lorry and went back to London Road. My other cousins Mary and Betty were there. Aunty said, "Let's have a look then". So I had to embarrass myself at a tender age in front of them all. One look and she said, "Take him to hospital". When we got there, two nurses looked at it and put eight stitches in. Even after 72 years I still get my leg pulled about it when I see my cousins. If it had been a few inches the other way I could have lost my manhood before I had ever started life.

Having done the journey on my own once, I then made it again nearly every school holiday until my 12th birthday. Then Mum and Dad bought me a racing bike for my birthday. I looked at the map and saw it was 74 miles by road to East Grinstead so I told my parents that I would ride it. They laughed and said, "You'll never make it". That made me even more determined.

On the map, the best route looked to be Alton to Guildford to Dorking to Reigate – fairly straighforward. So I left home at 0800 and started pedalling. But by the time I had got as far as Alton, I felt they were right - I would never make it. So I turned round and rode five miles back to Alresford where I went into a baker's shop and bought six current buns.

I sat on the edge of the kerb and ate them all, one after another. I said to myself, "I can do this" and I set off again and this time kept on going. I arrived in East Grinstead at 4:50 pm. It had taken me eight hours and 50 minutes – and I had done ten miles extra by riding back for my currant bun breakfast. After the holiday Uncle and Aunty would not let me ride back so I was taken to Three Bridges station and put on a train to Portsmouth with my bike, so I would only have to ride 20 miles home.

The route I had taken the first time was too hilly (I hadn't yet found out what the contour lines on the map meant) so in future I went via Petersfield, Midhurst, Billingshurst, Horsham and Crawley. I went up and back often and by the time I was 14, I had got the journey time down to three hours and 50 minutes. In the next year, before leaving school, I went up and back twice in the same day, having six hours rest when I arrived.

When on my school holidays up at East Grinstead I used to help Uncle Bert in another of his business ventures - chimney sweeping. We used to go to a lot of very big houses. On one occasion, the lady of the house came to the door of the very posh house and showed us into the room where the chimney had to be cleaned. She told the maid to keep an eye on us to make sure we made no dirt. Uncle closed the fireplace off and started putting the extending rods together and pushing them up the chimney. Then he asked me to go outside and to see if I could see the brush out of the top of the chimney. This I did a couple of times but couldn't see anything. He put the last rods on and said, "It has got to be out now". Just then, the door was flung open and the lady of the house stormed in. She said, "Mr Boyce, I asked you to sweep my chimney not clean my roses". What neither of us realised was that the very tall chimneys we could see were not the ones we were sweeping. On the other side of the house was a very short chimney and the brush had come out of the top and gone down among her roses.

Cricket can be a dangerous game

In the summer of 1950 a crowd of us boys decided to play cricket on a Saturday morning so off to the sports centre we went. We put three stumps one end for a wicket and one at the other and started to play. I was stood right next to the wicket when John came up to bowl against Trevor. He swung the bat as hard as he could and hit the ball but the bat came flying out of his hand at the same time hitting me in the mouth and knocking out my two front teeth. After that I had to get used to the kids singing "all he wants for Christmas is his two front teeth" whenever I left the house.

About nine months later I was at a bus stop with my friends and a smart gentleman kept looking in my direction. Suddenly he put his hand out and grabbed my lip. He said, "I am a dentist and can do something about this" and gave me his card. He said "Ask your mum to phone me." She did and made an appointment for me to see him. He fixed me a plate but it kept breaking as there were only two teeth supporting it, so he made me a stainless steel one which I still have today.

A young bird watcher

Around the same time, when I was twelve and a half, I was playing in the woods when I found a baby jackdaw. I took him home and fed him without much hope of him surviving, because he was so young but he pulled through and started to grow. We had a spare room in our house so I converted it into an aviary for him, with a perch. I opened up the window and put wire up to keep him in but used to let him out to fly around. When I went to the park on my bike he used to sit on my shoulder and I would let him fly around when we got there. To my surprise he always came back.

One day he was flying around and came in through the dining room window which was open while we were having dinner. My dad had just got home and had got into the habit of taking his false teeth out and putting them on the mantelpiece. The jackdaw saw them and picked them up in his beak. It looked as if he was laughing at us. Me and mum laughed as dad chased him round the room trying to catch him - I had shut the window so he could not get out.

A few weeks later my Jackdaw flew off and didn't return for some time. He was found about a mile away and I brought him home again. This happened a second time when he was about six months old..I let him out and on this occasion he never came back. I hoped he had found some of his own sort.

Tree Trouble

A friend told me that a man who lived in the same road had a big collection of birds eggs and had asked if we would like to go and see them the next day. He had an amazing collection of eggs of all different sizes and colours. He must have had about 100 of them. He told us that on Saturday he was going to the New Forest where he had been watching a woodpecker and invited us to go with him - so of course we all said yes.

We walked though the forest for some time until we came to a tree where he pointed up to a rough hole about 25 feet up. He said, "That's where she is. I need someone to climb up and get me an egg." I opened my big mouth and offered to have a go, so up I climbed. I was nearly there when I reached out and caught hold of a branch to pull myself up level with the nest. The branch was rotten and just came away and I went crashing to the ground. When I came to, gasping for breath the others were all around me telling me to just lay there and rest. I put my hands out, felt both sides of me and found there were hard roots of the tree protruding from the ground. Luckily I had not broken any bones but if I had landed on one of the roots instead of between them, I could have broken my back. As it was, I got away with a couple of bruises and a bad back for a few days.

Boys Brigade

In 1952, I went to camp with the Boys Brigade at Langton Matravers near Swanage. In the next field the Girls Brigade had their camp. The four boys in our tent decided to have some fun so on the second night we crept out after lights out at 10 pm. We had to be quiet because our officers were sat around the fire having a drink and talking. We climbed over the fence and let the guide ropes down on the girls' tent and ran. There was panic as the tent came down on the girls and they were screaming and running everywhere. We got back to our tent undetected and climbed back into our bunk beds. We could see a shadow of one of our officers going from tent to tent shining a very bright light into them. He came into our tent and shone his torch on us, one at a time. "Have you been out?" he demanded. We all said no and thought we had got away with it, but he then caught sight of one of the boy's shoes sticking out from under the bedclothes. The stupid lad had forgotten to take them off.

"At 6.30 am you will report to make breakfast," our officer told us and for the next two days we had to stay back to get lunch and dinner, peel all the vegetables and in between meals clean the site up. The officers' wives used to do all this. Now they went swimming and on walks with the rest. It taught us a lesson.

Above left: Alan Edward Rowe age 7 months,1938. Above right: Me enjoying the sea air, 1940.

My first means of transport – the first of many. My new trike in Summer 1945, aged 7.

On holiday in Bournemouth with mum and dad, July 1946.

The keen six-a-side football player in 1952.

With the Boys Brigade First Aid Shield in June 1952.

Me with mum and dad, and Prince our smooth-haired Collie in Swanage, 1954.

The working man. My first job working on a farm in the New Forest, 1953.

Chapter 2
The 1950s - Working for a Living

In years past the majority of people had one job all their lives but there are not many people now in that position. Today's average seems to be a little higher - around four or five jobs. But even judged by modern standards, my working life has been pretty exceptional as I have had 25 full-time jobs and 11 part-time jobs at various times.

The Farmer's Boy

My first job on leaving school in 1953 was on a small farm at Wilverley Post near Sway in the New Forest. We had six cows, two pigs, sows, and a chicken plus a cart horse and a riding horse.

Each morning I would milk the cows and then open the farm gate so the cows could go out into the forest. Then in the afternoon I used to walk about half a mile to find them. They were generally in a gulley where there was plenty of grass. I would give a whistle and they would look up and start coming back. But one day the Ayrshire did not come home so after milking the others I went looking for her and found her with a new-born calf. It had come about three weeks early otherwise we would have kept her in. I picked up the calf and carried it on my shoulders and around my neck and on the trip back the cow kept pushing into my back with her horns, so the next day I had a lot of bruising to my back.

I used to have to collect the morning papers each day. The railway line ran along the bottom of the farm and each day Smith's bookshop at Brockenhurst station would give the papers to the guard and he would throw them out to me on the embankment on his way to Ringwood and I would take them back to the big house. After breakfast I would have to get the horse ready for the master who went riding each day in the forest.

Farm Horse

Evenings on the farm were boring as there was no one to talk to, so I went down to the bottom field where our cart horse was kept and was fed each day. I would sit on the gate and he would come over to me. One night I stroked him a few times and decided I would ride him. So I went and got a rope, came back and put it round his neck then climbed on the gate to get on his back, when he made a bolt around the edge of the field with me hanging on for dear life. All down one edge of the field were branches hanging over from the woods and poking out. The horse tore under them and the next thing I knew was when I came to on the ground. When I looked up the horse was standing by me looking down with his big eyes and I could read in them what he was saying "That will teach you to ride me". I do not know how long I had been knocked out as a thick branch hit me across the chest but if it had been a bit higher it could have chopped my head off. I had bruising across the top of my body for about a week.

The cart horse was very crafty and could open the safety lock on the gate in the field she was in and then go out to join the ponies in the forest. Sometimes she was gone for a few days or even a couple of weeks and we would get phone calls telling us where she was.

We also had a sow who was due her litter. One morning I went to feed her and found she had broken out of her sty so I went looking for her. She had broken a large area of ferns down and put them in a pile and I could hear squeaking coming from it. When I removed some of the ferns there were 16 piglets fighting for her teats. We had to take some away and feed them by hand as she did not have enough teats.

Hay Making

It was hay making time on the farm when we had workers who cut the hay and stored it up on top of the hill. We used to harness the carthorse up to a hay cart with sides on it and when it was loaded, I used to sit on top of the hay and guide the horse with the reins in my hands up the hill. I did two trips up the narrow winding pathway without trouble but on the third trip my wheel must have come off the path, because I found myself flying through the air and landing up in a gorse bush with the hay and the cart on top of me. Luckily, the sides of the cart protected me – if it had been a flat wagon it could have crushed me. The farm hands released the horse and turned the cart upright. I was shocked and had bruising all over. I also spent the next few days pulling thorns from the gorse bush from all over my body.

I used to cycle the 18 miles from Southampton to the farm on a Sunday evening and back again Saturday lunchtime. What with that and the boredom, I packed this job in after nine months because it got so lonely. There was only me and Mr Gates who had been there for years living in a cottage in the grounds. The only other staff were part–time labourers hired when needed.

Ball Boy

In 1953, I went to see the cup tie between Blackpool and Southampton FC on the Saturday. The result was a draw, and the replay was set for midweek in the afternoon. There were no floodlights in those days and matches had to be played during the day. I was a bit late for the match and when I got there all the gates were closed. I decided I was not going all that way to Blackpool and then miss seeing the replay so I walked straight up to the players entrance as if I owned the place, said "Hello" to the doorman and added, "I will be in trouble I am late." I walked down the corridor which brought you out near the corner flag at the old Dell where four other men stood and I watched the match.

As the trick worked so well, for the next few weeks I did the same thing in 1969 – why pay when you can get in free. One Saturday Len Stadsbridge who was the ground keeper said, "Can you pick up the corner flags at end of game?" Of course, I jumped at the chance to be part of the team and I did it for the rest of the season. Then the following year I did the same. Then the person who collected the balls left so I took over his job. I had a big canvas bag into which they were stored and after the players had their warm up on the pitch they used to kick the balls to me and I would catch them in the bag and the crowd would give me a cheer. That is how I came to be ball boy at the Dell. It was a role I carried on playing

15

for many years – even when I later owned my own successful business. But that's a story for a later chapter.

My next job in 1953 was working as a shop assistant in Holts Newsagents and part of my job was to go out and deliver the papers if one of the paper boys did not turn up. I chucked it in after a year as I had to work on Saturday afternoon and that meant I could not play football, which was then very important to me. At the same time, from the age of 16, I started to work in night clubs for the next 20 years – part-time at first and full-time later. I worked behind the bar at the Astor Night Club, Carousel Club and the Rainbow Club amongst others.

Una Star Laundry

My next full-time job, in 1954, was at the Una Star Laundry as a packer putting all the linen laundry from ships in dock into hampers to be delivered back on board. It was here that I met my first love, Maureen. Every time I went to the canteen at Una Star I passed her. She worked on a press machine and it took me about a month to build up the courage to ask her out. Luckily she said yes. Two weeks later we were walking across the common. "Shall we lay down there in the long grass where no-one can see us," Maureen said. I knew we were going to make love. I had a pack of Durex with me as I was fully prepared it would happen some time. I was not quite 17 and Maureen was 16 and a half. "It's my first time," I said. "Me, too", she said. I got in such a tangle trying to put the rubber on and taking it off that I never used a condom again ever again in my life!

I also realised later that actually it wasn't Maureen's "first time", she had too much experience. Our relationship only lasted 8 months then, sadly, she met someone else.

I wanted to be out on the vans driving but the laundry would not allow it. The reason they gave me was that I was coming up to 18 and so I would soon be eligible for my national call up to the armed forces. I packed in the job because they wouldn't let me drive, but as it turned out, I failed my forces medical anyway.

The week before my medical was due, dermatitis broke out on both hands so when I went to the address I'd been given I had my hands done up as mittens. When I walked in the sergeant major saw me coming and started to laugh, saying to the medic, "Well, we've got a right one here." But when they removed the bandages they found my hands were all split and raw so I was failed on those grounds and also because I was colour blind. Two weeks after the medical, it had cleared up and I have never had it since. Shortly after, I left the laundry because I wanted to drive.

Next it was a job as a cook's assistant in a transport style café at the bottom of Lances Hill and Buller Road, serving on tables and kitchen. That really wasn't me and lasted only one week.

Una Star Again

In 1955 I went back to the Una Star as a laundryman under a different department and boss. I used to fill big machines with dirty washing and then take it out when finished. After three weeks working there my old boss came by and was surprised to see me there. By the end of the week he asked me if I would like to transfer to the transport side where I could go out driving. This was what I had wanted from the start, so of course I said yes.

On the driving side I started on bag wash rounds - where people would put their dirty washing in a bag, you would collect it and return it the next day. There was also delivering hampers of linen to big houses, hotels and firms.

One day I was driving the bag wash van and had to call on a house at the bottom of a narrow lane near the Ice House Pub in Shirley Warren. It had been raining hard for a few days and I was halfway down the lane but unknown to me the rain had washed half the bank away and the van suddenly toppled on its side where the bank had been. There was a drop on my nearside and a lake below but on its bank were many small trees that held the van up and stopped it from sliding into the lake.

My career as the most accident-prone man carried on shortly after when I was delivering hampers with clean sheets and tablecloths to the Balmer Lawn Hotel in the New Forest. The hotel had an outdoor lift for goods at the back. I used to load the hampers onto the lift then I would go up to the third floor to take them off and put on the dirty ones for return. The lift was worked by pulling on a rope and when it got to your floor level you stopped it with a brake. I had opened the doors and lifted the hampers off and reloaded it ready to go down. I started to lower it but I could not have been holding tight enough because the rope started tearing into my hands and the next thing I knew I had been pulled off the floor and was hanging over the lift shaft. I managed to swing myself back on to the floor. I felt no pain at the time but when I looked down there was blood everywhere and skin was hanging from my hands. I went to A&E at Lymington Hospital where they bathed them and put ointment on them then they told me to come back in two days' time. They warned me I might have to have skin grafts but when I went back they said I would be OK. I had to keep bandages on for two weeks so I walked around looking like a boxer with his gloves on.

A brilliant idea

Not long after I passed my driving test, I had what I thought was a brilliant idea for a new business venture. My uncle Bert in East Grinstead had packed up his wood business and for two years or so had been vacuum chimney sweeping. He'd been successful so I thought I'd try my hand at it too. The process was simple enough. You put a screen on the fire place and sealed it, attached the hose to the bottom and sucked up the loose soot as you swept. What could go wrong?

I bought an old van and the vacuum on finance, got an old ladder and stuck it on top of the van and painted "Rowvax" on the side. On my first day I put the brush up the chimney and tried to pull it down but I must have turned the rod the wrong way because the brush head came off and stayed stuck up the chimney. So I cleaned up, collected my money and left. A couple of weeks later the same thing happened. This time, I had a plan. I lit a newspaper, let the wind take it up the chimney. There was a roar and into the hearth fell the head of the brush with its bristles burnt off.

I realised that chimney sweeping wasn't as easy as it looked, so I turned to window cleaning. One lady with a big house phoned me up for a quote. I asked her how many windows and gave her a price. She said she would be out but would leave the money under the mat – that was the sort of thing people did in those days. When I arrived I saw the windows were all of the lattice style – a lot more work than I had bargained for. But I got on with the job. Then I found the next snag. They had a large glass conservatory and two of the windows were above it. As I tried to move the ladder into position I put it through one pane of glass. So I collected my money and went and never heard from her again.

As well as problems like this I also ran into trouble with BT. I had been leaving my calling cards in the telephone boxes in Southampton and they wrote to me threatening to take me to court. I decided this was not the job for me so I packed it in after four weeks.

After this spell of self-employment, I was taken on as a pipe fitter's mate for Husband's Shipyards at Marchwood. The firm had a contract to replace the pipework on the cracker at Fawley refinery. Each day we would clock on, then a lorry would take us out to the refinery and bring us back at tea time. The working process was very boring . We would start by having a breakfast break then I would go with a pipe fitter to measure up some pipe. We then gave measurements to a welder who would cut pipe and weld flanges onto it, while we sat down and made tea again. Then next day we would contact the rigger to have this piece put into place. I would then bolt it to hold it together. That would take two days for one simple job.

There were also rules. If they had an urgent job we would work on until it was finished. If it took up to midnight they would supply a hot meal and if it went over midnight we had the next day off with pay. We were taken to a café down by the old refinery gates on one occasion and when we had finished the café owner asked, "Who is going to pay?" Big mouth me shouted out, "Charge Husband's". When we returned to work after our day off I went to clock in but there was no card for me, so I went to see the foreman who told me Jack Husband wanted to see me. The men all went off to the site but I had to stay behind and wait. When Mr Husband arrived he accused me of being a trouble maker at the café the night before and he fired me. I went out to the site and told the foreman. He got all the men to down tools. Negotiations went on for two days. First they would re-employ me but not pay the men for the time when they had downed tools. In the end they gave in to everything. I got my job back but I didn't like working under union rules so I went after about 4 months.

Taxi Driver

From 1956 to 1957 I drove taxis for a man named Jimmy Hobbs. He didn't pay well, and the job meant working all hours but I was happy even though I was earning only half what I did on my last job. I suppose I could say that what my job with Jimmy lacked in financial rewards, it more than made up for with adventures of one kind or another.

Jimmy had two taxis and his office was on Redbridge Hill and as most of our trade was in town I used to sit in the Lord Roberts pub and he would phone when he had a customer for me. One such night, about 10 pm, it was raining hard as I sped toward West Quay Road and at the end turned left to go in the Docks. I hit the brakes and the car shot forward, aquaplaned on the wet road and I smashed into the fence opposite where Southampton Car Auctions used to be. Luckily I got away lightly. All I had was bruising, a strained wrist and shock

Shortly after there was snow and ice on the ground. As I was on my way to the taxi rank at Shirley and came down Church Street, which is on an incline, I touched the brakes the car shot forward, slid sideways on the ice and at that moment another taxi turned the corner and I went straight into him. It was only then I realised it was our other cab. So now both cars would be off the road for repair. This time I had more bruises, shock plus a cut on my forehead.

The weather improved and one night I had a call to the Platform Tavern at Town Quay where the landlady wanted me to take an American back to his boat just inside number four gate of the docks. He was so drunk he could hardly stand up and I had to help him into the cab. I wasn't happy about the state he was in and told the landlady if he was sick in the car I would come back for compensation as I would be off the road while I cleaned it up. I only had to take my drunk fare round the park and into the docks so it wasn't a long journey. The minimum fare in those days for the first mile was one shilling and ninepence but I decided he was a lot more trouble so I charged him a dollar - worth seven shillings then.

It was high tide and the boat towered above us. The gangway went almost vertically up on the ship's side. I managed to get him out of the cab and leant him against it. It was pretty dark as there were no lights and eventually he paid me. I watched him stagger up the gangway, scared that he would fall and kill himself, but with the luck of drunks he made it to the top. I then went back to the pub and told the landlady he had been sick and got her to cough up £3.

When I got home that night I emptied all the money onto the table and worked out how much to pay the boss and how much were my tips. I had only taken one American dollar bill that night and I picked it up meaning to put it to one side when I realised it was a $100 bill worth £70. I did not go into a bank to change it until the boat had sailed.

When I was driving taxis for Jimmy Hobbs I would occasionally get a call from attractive ladies to take them from their homes to a pub in the city centre, and then take them back home later in the evening. Often they were accompanied back by a gentleman who always paid the fare. Of course, it was none of my business what my customers did, but it was true to say that some of them lived in an area of the city that had a certain reputation.

On one occasion, one of my ladies – let's call her Polly – called a taxi from the pub and travelled home alone. When we arrived at her flat she said, "Would you like to stay the night? It's late, and I'm lonely." As she was my last fare for the night, I accepted her kind offer.

In the morning, Polly made breakfast and I was just about to leave when we heard a racket from the street outside. I looked down from her first floor flat just in time to see my taxi being driven off down the street. Of course, I immediately called the police and told them my taxi had been stolen. They arrived promptly and within 20 minutes I was making a statement to a constable. At that moment my boss Jimmy Hobbs arrived in another taxi with a policeman. He was red-faced as he had to explain that he had taken my taxi to teach me a lesson, because I had parked it outside all night. The police were not at all happy about this but legally he was in the right as it was his car.

When the police had gone, Jimmy said, "I'll take you to pick up your taxi." But as we got going he said, "Don't let me catch you parking in Cranbury Road all night again – you don't know what could happen to the car." Cranbury Road and the surrounding streets had a reputation as being somewhat less than law-abiding.

A few days later, fate dropped into my lap the perfect opportunity to get my own back on Jimmy. I was dropping off a customer in Dunkirk Road late at night and I spotted Jimmy's car parked under some trees near a row of prefabs. I pulled up to log my last fare of the evening and as I sat there I saw Jimmy come out of a gate on the other side of the road and walk to his car. I looked at my watch and it was 1:10 am. Jimmy was seeing a woman. Knowing Jimmy and seeing the lateness of the hour, I guessed she was married.

It was a Tuesday night when I spotted him so I went back the next Tuesday night at a quarter past midnight and sure enough his car was parked outside again. I switched my engine off and coasted silently to the gate. I got out, made a noise fumbling with the gate, stamped loudly down the path and made a noise with the letter box like someone fumbling with the door. Then I legged it back to my car and drove off quickly.

Next morning early I got a call from Jimmy asking me to go to his home before going to the taxi rank at Shirley. He told me to park outside his flat which was unusual because I normally went in to say hello to his wife. After a few minutes he came out, opened the passenger door and put a jacket and trousers on the seat. They were covered in mud.

"What have you been up to?" I asked innocently.

He said, "Take them to a 24-hour cleaners, will you – only I got caught out last night. I'm seeing a woman whose husband is on nights and last night he came home early. When we were just about to make love, we heard the gate open and footsteps coming down the path. I grabbed my clothes, climbed out of the window and had to climb across three gardens to get back to my car." I just nodded sympathetically.

Mavis

Life went on. In my spare time I used to go to the dances at the Palmerston ball rooms and the Royal Pier where Gillie Humes' band played. One night two of us went to the Empire Hall at Totton for a change. It was just after I had passed my driving test and bought my first car, aged 17 and a half. I remember it now, an Austin 16 with running boards down the side. When the dance finished a lot of friends wanted a lift home. You had plenty of friends if you had a car then. So we tried to see how many people we could get into it and we managed to cram in 12. I was sat sideways steering, with someone else changing gear when I told them to. There were four of us in the front and eight in the back. That was the night I met Mavis for the first time.

A few weeks later I met her again and we started going out together. One day I met her from her work at Woolworth's in Shirley and we walked along Shirley High Street. I stopped outside a jewellers shop window and said, "Do you like any of those rings?" I thought she looked shocked, but we went in and without having even thought about it bought a ring. When I had got out of bed that morning I had no intention to get engaged at the age of 18.

That was the high point of a very special day. But later that evening we were driving into town to celebrate when I had a terrible accident which ruined our perfect day. It's still very painful to think about sixty years on.

I picked Mavis up in Foundry Lane and cut up a side street and turned right to go into Town. I was doing less than 30 miles per hour and had just passed Shirley Police Station when a woman ran out between two parked cars. I did not have time to brake and hit her. She was thrown up in the air and crashed onto the ground. I sent my girlfriend back home and waited with the woman until the police and ambulance came to take her away. The police immediately tested my brakes and found them working perfectly. Two weeks later I picked up a copy of the Southern Echo and found the full story about the woman who had died after being hit by a car two weeks earlier, and knew it referred to my accident. Two days later the police called and told me that no actions would be taken against me. They said that the poor woman suffered from epileptic fits and may have been having one when I hit her because she had bad burns where she had fallen into the fireplace at home.

Marriage

During this time, I was still seeing Mavis regularly since our engagement. In 1956 we decided to get married. We had nowhere to live but my father, knowing we had no money to our name, changed our house around so we could have three rooms to start us off. About three weeks before the big day I started to worry that I could not go through with it as was expected of me. Everyone around me tried to offer reassurance. "That's just normal wedding nerves" they said. But I had a gut feeling something was not right. All the while we courted I was never invited into her house – not even after we were married. I had never met her parents.

The big day arrived and I got to the church ready, my best man at my side. Mavis did not arrive on time and the later it got the more I wished I had the courage to call it off but the reception was waiting and some people had come a long way. Half an hour later she arrived and I found out later that her parents had been up the pub. I guess they were getting their fix because the reception was in the adjoining church hall, with no alcohol allowed. Once it was all over we were off to Blackpool for our honeymoon.

I carried on working at several jobs to keep us afloat, then Mavis became pregnant after 10 months and before we knew it we were holding our first born, a girl we called Sharon. I was only 20 years old. A second child was born a year later. We named her Yvonne.

Long distance

My endless job-hunting continued. First, I became a bus conductor on Hants & Dorset buses which had the open platform at the back, travelling local journeys and also longer bus routes to Calshot, Petersfield and Winchester.

Life as a conductor was fun as I came into contact with people but I missed being my own boss as a driver out on the road. So I went back to long distance driving. First it was running sherry from William and Herbert at Testwood up to Glasgow and later similar work for Victory Transport.

A Huge Blow

In 1958 something happened that changed my whole life. I was working the night shift at A. C. Delco at Southampton docks, a maker of metal parts for cars. Sometimes I worked on presses and sometimes operated a lathe. One night I was working as a press operator in a very noisy shop floor and the Tannoy was bellowing somebody's name out over and over. Then I realized it was my name. I rushed over to the manager and he handed me the phone. It was Mavis. "Come home Alan. Dad has passed away." I could not believe what I was hearing: he was only 44 years old. When I got home, Mum said, "Do you want to go and see him?" The bedroom was down along the passage. I just stood there staring at the door for what seemed ages before I could go in. And when I did he looked so peaceful.

I then had to get a taxi over to his mother's to tell her and his brother about his death. I had to get to the house before Hedley went to work, where he worked with dad. I knocked on the door and told him and he said, "You will have to go up to Grandma's bedroom and tell her, I can't." Dad also had a sister Lilly and within a year both she and Grandma died. People reckon Lilly pined for her brother and Grandma could not bear it that she had lost a son and daughter as well as losing her husband in the war.

A few weeks later I found out that Mavis was pregnant again and I still felt unsure about our relationship. I don't know why but I just wanted to be free. I never got on with my dad much and it was only when he was gone that I realized how much I loved him and I was angry and hated him for leaving me.

Show Business

In 1958 my career changed direction in a big way. The SS "Ivernia" was holding a dance at the Top Hat ballroom in Dorset Street while the ship was in port and the music was being provided by a group called "The Sunsets" that was made up of crew members. They asked me if I would become their manager and get work for them when they were in port.

They also planned to play while their ship was sailing, in the lounge after their day's work was done. But the captain told them they couldn't play like that as the musician's union had kicked up a fuss – the crew's band was so good that nobody was going in the ballroom. So the group decided to come ashore permanently and try to make a go of it in the music industry. They changed their name to the "Transatlantic Seven". We later dropped the "Seven" because if anyone left the group it would saddle us with the problem of finding a replacement. So they became "Transatlatic" and that went down well with the customers.

As I now had a band to manage, I decided I might as well open my own agency. I called it Alan Rowe Entertainments and I took an office above John Beirne's music shop in Shirley. I started to put on big beat nights at the Guildhall and eight-hour non-stop beat from 3pm to 11pm each Sunday at the Bannister Ballroom. I also used the Tower Ballroom at Lee on Solent, the Lido, Winchester, and the Drill Hall at Fareham and Lymington. I also put on a big show for all the paper boys and girls as a thank you for all the bad weather they had worked through and was booked by Mr Holt who was chairman of the Southampton Newsagents Group.

Artists who performed at my shows included big names like Jean Vincent, Sounds Incorporated, The Barron Knights, The Downland Brothers with The Soundtracks, Betty Smith with her Quintet, Billy Fury, The Merseybeats, Eddie Cochrane and many more. My own band the Transatlantics appeared on most shows to showcase them to audiences. The Transatlantics were getting known and the area they played in was spreading. One day we covered for Cliff Bennett and the Rebel Rousers who had an accident and we tore down to the Mecca Ballroom at Plymouth at short notice to take their place.

On one occasion I hired Southampton Guildhall for the night to put on a big dance with star names providing the music. The hall had a very strict policy on numbers and would only allow 1,000 people in for dancing. To enforce the policy they had an attendant seated near the entrance with a hand-held clicker. When he reached the limit he would stop the promoter from allowing in any more visitors. On the night we had a huge crowd turn out and I could see he was reaching the limit on his clicker. I looked outside and saw there was still a long queue of hundreds of people stretching down the road. I went to the entrance desk, took a £20 note from the cash drawer and went to have a word with the attendant. I poked the note into his top pocket and told him, "There aren't many people outside now – you might as well go and get yourself a drink." The gentleman was glad to be relieved of his boring job – and we got nearly another 500 through the door at 7 shillings and sixpence a ticket.

My entry to the entertainment business was going well but I then made a big mistake. I went into partnership with a fellow called Reg Marshall and this led to problems for me. Behind my back he got the Transatlantics to sign a contract with him. When he told me I was so shocked and angry I told him to get out of my office. I could not believe the boys could do this to me. I had put every penny I had to get them somewhere. I had bought some of their equipment in my name, as well as a minibus and I even had an audition for a record company in the pipeline. If they were successful they would have got a record contract with an appearance on TV shows like Oh Boy and the Six Five Special. They threw it all away. I heard that they had been told that I was making money out of them and not giving them a fair share – the opposite of the truth. If they had come to me and talked it over I would have shown them the paper trail that proved where the money went. I was so shocked and hurt by this that I became disillusioned with the music industry and I packed it in. But that was one of the big mistakes I made in my life - I should have carried on.

Instead I went back to long-distance driving again. I then moved on to Reeves Transport from Manchester, although I worked out of their Southampton depot. Many of the runs would be local but then I would take my turn at night driving to Manchester. However we organised it so that I would meet a lorry coming south and change over at a car park at Warwick. That way I could sleep in my own bed after a long trip. I then did similar work for Smith of Maddison from Scotland doing mostly long distance like bringing steel down from Glasgow.

So that was how the 1950s came to an end, with me having covered more thousands of miles up and down the country than I can count. I suppose like everyone else I celebrated the new year wondering what the new decade would bring. If I had known, I might not have celebrated quite so much.

Above: *I move from three wheels to four. At Cheddar Gorge with my first set of wheels in 1956.*

Below: *With mum and dad in the New Forest in 1959.*

I finally get my dearest wish – I become a driver with the Una Star Laundry, with my own van! 1957

Above: Trying out my new uniforms as both driver and conductor for the Hants and Dorset Bus Company. 1958

Below Left: Me with Prince in the garden in 1954. **Below Right:** I think I must have just bought a new suit. Looking smart , in 1962.

.

Chapter 3
1960s - The Swinging Sixties

When 1960 dawned, I took one of the biggest decisions of my life. I decided to leave Mavis with the two children and another one on the way. I was 22 years old. Of course, everybody ran me down for leaving and, to tell the truth, I did not blame them. But I knew in my heart that it was inevitable. If I had not gone then, it would have happened later.

I felt sorry for mum as she was now left in her house with my wife and children. Mavis hated me which is natural and would not let me see the children. So I went to court to get access and the court ruled that I must be allowed to see them. But every time I arranged to, she would shut the door in my face or not answer the door at all.

Mum sold the large house and moved to a smaller one. One day I called to see her and my two daughters were visiting their grandma. When they went home they told their mummy that they had seen me. Mavis's response was to tell mum that if I saw them once more she would never have the children again. So after that I had no choice but to make sure I stayed away when they were visiting. A few years later Mavis married again and then I received a legal notice that her new husband wanted to adopt them. People asked me how could I possibly agree but again I felt I had little choice. Mavis would not let me see them, and the children needed a stable home. On top of that, it was costing me a lot of money in maintenance payments – often more than I could afford – and the law was tougher on fathers then.

On one occasion I had got behind for a few months and decided I had better pay some of the arrears. I went into the civic centre, saw the official concerned and handed some money over the counter to him. The gentleman behind the counter checked his books and asked me to wait a minute. The next thing I felt was a hand on my shoulder. I looked behind me and found a big policeman who took me to Winchester prison. In those days you were imprisoned for arrears of maintenance. I was supposed to spend 14 days in jail but was released after three days inside because my then employer, Bill Summerfield, paid my back maintenance.

I'll never forget those three days. During my time inside I learned how to split a match four ways . I hated every moment of it and am sure now that most people – no matter how small the crime - who served two weeks inside with no TV, no phone, or no exercise, would never go back.

The early years of the 1960s were spent continuing as a long-haul lorry driver, taking every kind of goods the length and breadth of Britain.

Over loaded 1960

I was driving for Victory Transport in 1960 and had taken a load of sherry from Williams and Humbert at Teswood up to Port Dundas near Glasgow. When I was empty I loaded lead ingots and some steel plates 3'x2'wide and a box 3'x2'square which had to be delivered on the journey home at Watford. I had two thirds of a load and had to pick up the rest at Sutton Coldfield near Birmingham.

I left Glasgow early in the morning and the place I was going to put my lorry on the weighbridge so they could work out how many roofing tiles they could load me up with to my maximum weight. After loading up, I carried on driving until I got near Stratford-Upon-Avon and pulled into a layby. I didn't want to spend the night in a bed and breakfast place but decided to get some sleep in the lorry because I wanted to leave soon after midnight so I could get down to Watford and be waiting outside the factory when they opened in the morning. I wanted to get rid of the steel box so I could get home to see Southampton's first match of the season.

I was now going to go across country via Bicester and Aylesbury and I was only a few miles outside Stratford when I came to a very steep hill with u-bends. I was half way up and in first gear when the lorry stopped. I pulled my handbrake on and put my foot down on the foot brake but the lorry started to go backwards. There was a steep drop on my offside and a bank on my nearside. I was on one of the u-bends and knew if I did nothing I would go straight over and topple down the drop so I swung the wheel so the lorry crashed into the bank.

The next thing I knew the lorry had gone up the bank and then came down and skewed right across road on its side. I was shaken, but scrambled out. Just then a car came round the bend and screeched to a halt. The driver offered to run back up the hill to wave down other vehicles before there was an accident. And there was a house at the top of the hill from where he called the police,

When they arrived they called a recovery truck who tried to pull the lorry upright but it was too heavy. I told the police they would have to get a stronger vehicle, but they said that would take too long and they had to clear the road as soon as possible. They told me, "The only solution is we will have to cut your ropes."

Up to then my load was still intact with the ropes and tarpaulin holding it in place. But as soon as they cut the ropes the metal pipes bounced down the road and the roofing tiles scattered everywhere. Once we'd got the lorry upright again, we then had to reload the goods except the roofing tiles which were shovelled up and swept over the embankment. The police then took me back to their station. It was 4 am and I told them I could not call my office till it opened the next morning at 8 am so they told me, "You can sleep in a cell". I didn't get much sleep that night because they weren't supposed to let me sleep there and their sergeant came on duty at 6:30 am so they woke me at 6:00.

I went with them to a transport café about three miles away where we got some breakfast. I phoned the office and they sent a lorry up to transfer the rest of load. When it arrived at 11.30am it was driven by my mate Brian.

We then drove to the recovery yard and transferred what was left of the load and returned to Southampton. I never did see Saints' first match. I was suspended from driving so I had to work in the warehouse while they investigated what caused the accident. After three days I was back driving. They found out the roofing tile people had made a mistake and had overloaded me by three tons. No wonder the lorry would not go uphill.

Another overload

Not long after I had another experience with a heavily-laden lorry. It was an eight-wheeled Foden belonging to Reeves Transport and I had loaded 20 tons of rubber onto it at Monsanto at Fawley Refinery. I drove this to Membury near Newbury, to an old RAF station where the rubber was being stored in the hangers.

I had just passed the Beaulieu Road turn-off and got to the top of the incline down to the Hythe roundabout. As I was approaching the roundabout, I put my foot on the brake and it went straight to the floor. The brakes had failed completely I blew the horn and switched my lights on as the lorry started going faster and faster. I could not change gear because the gear box was not synchronised like modern ones. The last thing I saw before I hit the roundabout was a Mini Traveller which I hit up the back and which shot round the roundabout like a rocket. When I came to, I was upside down in the lorry and men were trying to lift me out of the cab. I was taken to Lymington Hospital where they checked me over. I had bruising all over my body and a couple of cuts. They kept me in overnight as a precaution. I later learned that the ministry officer checking over the lorry found the footbrake had come off the spline which, of course, it was not supposed to do.

Threatening Behaviour

One night in 1962 I was driving a lorry back from London and decided to stop and try and see my kids in Southampton. I went to the door but, as usual, Mavis would not let me see them. As I turned to leave, the next door neighbour - a former sergant-major about a foot taller than me - leaned over the fence from next door and gave a sarcastic grin. Mum had had trouble with him in the past, so I tried to ignore him. When I reached the gate he said sarcastically "Won't she let you see them?" As I stepped onto the pavement, I turned and put my finger up to threaten him and he stepped back and fell straight through the fence. I turned away and crossed the road to get in my lorry when I heard a noise behind me.

He was coming at me with a brick in his hand, but in his hurry he fell over. I went back and dragged him onto the pavement before he got run down. As I drove away he started banging on the side of the motor. He took me to court for assault and I was found guilty because I threatened him with my finger!

One Arm Bandit

When I drove for Victory Transport we used to load crates containing "one arm bandit" gambling machines at Southampton docks. In those days gaming machines were very strictly controlled. They arrived every week aboard the liners Queen Mary and Queen Elizabeth from New York. They were unloaded and stored in a customs bonded cage at the end of the Ocean Terminal until we were told to collect them. Then, three customs officers would open up the cage and supervise us loading them onto the lorry. Once I had loaded the crates, a customs officer would travel with me to our depot at Rownhams, where the lorry would be locked in a warehouse for the night. Next morning, the officer would meet me and travel to London with me.

On my second trip, I said to the customs officer, "It's silly you coming to our depot. I can drop you off in Shirley and pick you up next morning". He accepted my offer because it saved him waiting around for buses to get home.

With a normal load you had three crates across the bed of the lorry with twelve rows of crates along the length. And there was also a second tier of crates on top – making 72 crates in all. I had worked out that if I spread the outside crates in the bottom tier out a bit but pushed the inside ones hard together, I could get one extra crate inside. When the second tier was in place it looked like there was a crate missing, even though all 72 were loaded. So that was how I arranged them next time I carried a load.

The customs officer said, "That's your lot." But I replied, "No I need one more." He and two other officers then carefully counted the crates again, down the sides and across the ends and in the row on top and they also came up with one short.

My officer said, "Someone on the ship must have signed for them but didn't check that there was one short." I roped the load and put a tarpaulin over them. Before leaving I told the customs man I was just going to phone my wife to tell her what time I'd be home for tea. Instead I phoned a mate of mine who had a van and who I had arranged with in advance where we could meet.

I dropped the officer off near his home, drove round to the back of Nurseling, untied the ropes and unloaded a crate onto my mate's van. Then I drove onto Rownhams as usual. In the evening we got rid of the crate by breaking it up so it could not be traced. I then phoned the boss of a nightclub I had worked at and asked him if he wanted an extra machine. In those days no establishment could have more than one machine by law, but I knew he was a bit of a rogue and would go for it. I asked £250 and told him at 6 pence a pull he would soon get his money back. He beat me down to £220, so I delivered it to him. I gave my mate £20 which was nearly a week's wages.

By 1962 I had had enough of long distance driving for the time being, so I went to work full time at the Carousel Night Club for Bob Fagan. Instead of sitting behind a wheel, I was doing bar work and waiting in the restaurant. I had been a regular customer in the Carousel for years and had sometimes helped out behind the bar when they were busy. Now going to work there full time proved to be the start of a whole series of jobs and a whole new life.

At the Carousel, I would go in, stock up the bar and deal with the empties. Bob also ran the Top Hat Ballroom above where we used to do functions and weddings as well as men-only nights – which often ended up in the newspapers. I acted as the floor manager for all the functions up there making sure the waitresses served and cleared the tables when needed.

Some of the Southampton Football Club players used to come into the Carousel night club and one memorable Friday night legendary centre forward Ron Davies came in. I think Ron must have been celebrating something big because by the time we closed at 1 am he was very, very drunk. I helped him out and got him a taxi. I opened the door and he crawled into the back seat but as I closed it he crawled out of the other door. Eventually I got him in and saw him safely off, wondering how on earth he would manage next day, Saturday. But at 3 pm next day he was on the pitch playing in an international for Wales, running, jumping up and heading the ball as usual. How he could even run I don't know after the night before. His favourite drink was dark rum and blackcurrant, which I expect he is drinking up in the sky and looking down on us. Well done Ron. You were a great centre forward.

A Late Night Encounter

As well as night clubs in Southampton, I also used to visit clubs in other towns. One I visited more than once was a club in Bournemouth that used to stay open until 1 am. On Friday and Saturday nights after it was closed to the public the owner used to let groups and bands who had been playing in the area come in and get up on the stage and play, until around 4 am. This meant driving home on deserted roads in the early hours of the morning. I drove via Christchurch and the New Forest and one night in 1964 I had just passed the Rhinefield House turn off when something white came across my windscreen and smashed it.

I hit the grass verge and flipped over into a ditch. Luckily for me a man on his way to work saw what had happened and helped me. He told me he was driving round the bend when he saw my headlights disappear. He knew there was no turning off so he slowed down and saw my car. An ambulance arrived and I was taken to Lymington Hospital where they checked me over. I had bruising and concussion so they kept me in for 24 hours as a precaution.

During the day two policemen came to see me and asked what happened. I told them I thought it may have been a white deer. They laughed and said the only animals in the forest that were white were a couple of horses. A few days later I read in the local Echo about a white stag who was found dead in a swamp near where my accident occurred. The story stated the stag could not get out of the swamp because of injuries it had sustained by being hit by a vehicle. I knew it was me and felt like going to Lymington police station and saying to the two officers, "There - I told you so".

As well as working in the Carousel, I also continued to do some taxi work to make ends meet. Often it meant a lot of tedious waiting around, but on occasions it became "interesting."

Taxi Adventures

I was on the rank at Ogle Road one hot summer night about 9 pm when the back door opened and someone got in. I looked in my interior mirror and saw a good looking woman. "Where to?" I said. "Testwood please driver," she said. So we started our trip past the Railway Station and down Millbrook Road. Suddenly I heard her sigh and say, "That's better." When I looked she had stripped off and said, "Would you like to stop for a while?"

I never said no to sex and was not going to miss this opportunity with the good looking lady. I think she was about 25 years old. So I pulled into a lane opposite the end of Regents Park Road which led down to the shore where some small boats were tied up and pulled up on the shingle which nowadays has been reclaimed for the container port.

We spent 45 minutes there then got dressed and I drove her home. I had left the taximeter ticking over all the time and felt if she wanted me she would have to pay for the pleasure. She then asked if I would be on the rank the following Sunday at 9 pm. I said yes, I was there but she never showed. Pity because she was a very good lay.

Around this time I would wait for fares on the cab rank at 107 berth at the docks. Of course, we drivers all hoped we would get a long fare and cursed our luck when the customer only wanted a short trip. Passengers began to appear when a ship docked from Cowes on the Isle of Wight and its passengers were being brought over to Southampton by tender. When I got to the head of the rank I found my fares were two Americans - an older man and a younger. They walked out of the shed with no cases so I knew it wasn't my day– they would only be going local.

When they got in I asked, "Where to?" They said they were going to London and wanted me to take them to the coach station. It was 10:30 am in the morning. I knew there wouldn't be another coach until 2 pm. So I offered to take them all the way to London for £5. The younger man turned down my offer. All the way to the coach stop he kept telling his friend how he had been here two years earlier, how he knew all the ropes and how to watch out for locals on the make from unwary Americans. He obviously included me in this category. I was getting so fed up with his bragging I could not wait to get there. When they got out at the coach station, he said "How much, driver?" I said "Four and sixpence". He peeled off four £1 notes and handed them to me with a sixpence. With all his bragging he did not know a thing. He wouldn't pay £5 to be taken all the way London but paid me £4 and sixpence instead of 4 shillings and sixpence. His money was not going to last long. If he had not been so unfriendly I would have pointed out his mistake. As it was I felt it served him right.

Coach Driver

In 1962 I joined Summerfields Hire Service – in the end this turned out to be one of the best moves I ever made, as you'll see. At Summerfields I did private and contract hire with a minibus as well as driving a taxi.

Then Jack Jacobs, who owned a coach company, asked me to join his staff full time. This was an important break for me as a young driver because Jack put me through my PSV (Public Service Vehicle operator's license). This is the license that you must have in order to carry passengers on vehicles such as coaches and buses. I was the only qualified driver with the company full time.

I did private hire work in and around Southampton and then began driving to Europe, going to Paris, Amsterdam, Brussels and the Le Mans 24-hour motor race. Then for the next two summers I drove backwards and forwards to a camp site in Spain at Malgrat–de–Mar. There was no Autoroute on the journey, just ordinary roads. The first leg was the car ferry from Southampton to Cherbourg then 150 miles to our first overnight stop in Laval, next 400 miles to Toulouse and for our second night finished across border and onto the campsite arriving about 2 pm. Each trip meant travelling out for two and a half days, followed by a nine day break and then doing the same journey in reverse.

After driving umpteen thousand miles for Jack Jacobs, I had an argument with him and left. Five months later he knocked on my door one day and asked if I would go to Spain to bring back some passengers and the coach that were stranded because the driver had flown home. I said yes, and did rescue the passengers but I did not go back to work for him after. However, we stayed the best of friends going on holidays together and travelling to functions around the world. And this relationship eventually paid off in the most unexpected way.

Stormy weather

The experience of functions and restaurant work that I gained there meant that in 1964 I joined Thoresen Car Ferries sailing aboard their flagship, Viking II The officers were all Norwegian and we were employed as staff who could be switched around from job to job. I started out as a silver service waiter in the restaurant where it was a buffet and you could eat as much as you liked from Southampton to Cherbourg for seven shillings and sixpence. In the winter when we were slack I was switched to the kitchen where I filled the racks and then put them on a conveyor belt to go through the dish washer. We worked four days on and two off.

One night in 1964, on Viking II coming back from Le Havre, France, we hit a Force 9 to 10 gale as soon as we left harbour. We were being thrown all over the place and I was seriously worried that we might capsize as the ferries were so flat bottomed. To make matters worse, a Mayday call came in that a yacht was in distress so the Norwegian officers decided to try and help her.

The SS France was in ahead of us but it would take her about three miles before she could start to turn round even if she was able to turn in the heavy seas and bad weather. As we came up into a crest of a wave we could see the yacht and two people holding onto the mast. We then went down in a trough and when we came back up there was a helicopter with two people dangling from a ladder underneath but no sign of their boat. They had been plucked to safety in the nick of time.

Later Viking I passed us riding with the storm where we were against it and she called over on her Tannoy, "It's about time you got your bottom cleaned." We waved to her and carried crashing through the waves We arrived in Southampton two hours late with nearly all the crockery smashed, chairs piled up on top of one another and sick everywhere. Our Norwegian officer said, "We'll clean the ship up and leave again at 1 am instead of 10 pm" but the crew refused and said they wanted a night home after what we had been through. We said we would return ready to leave at 7 am the next day, and that's what we did.

It was back to coach driving after that, but the good and the bad luck still followed me everywhere.

Shattering Windscreen

In 1966, I was taking a Jacobs International Coach to London for an evening football match between Tottenham Hotspur and Southampton Football Club and had picked up stewards and landlords from pubs in Southampton. I had got to the top of the Avenue and was driving down Hut Hill at around 65 miles per hour when there was an almighty bang and the whole windscreen came in on me. It would not happen today because the glass is made to shatter into small pieces now. I managed to pull up safely but there were cuts all over my face and hands and blood everywhere. I then drove slowly up to Leigh Road till I came to the Pirelli factory and went into the security office where I phoned Ken Pitter of Colisseum Coaches to get a replacement coach to take the passengers on to London. The security guard then showed me to the factory first aid room where they cleaned me up and put three stitches in the cuts. I was surprised that none of the passengers were cut because when I was sweeping the coach out next day I found glass half way down the aisle.

An "Interview" with the Police

In 1966 I took a coach trip with schoolchildren up in the Lake District for eight days. They were staying at a youth hostel and I was staying in a pub a mile down the road at Ulverston. Each day I would take them out, drop them one side of a mountain and pick them up miles away on the other side, as they were on a hiking and climbing break.

On the Saturday and Sunday I got quite friendly with the young lads and their girls in the pub and on the Monday evening they said they were all going to a dance in the golf club on Thursday,

It was about three miles away, and invited me to go with them. I asked "How many of you are going?" They said about 25 so I suggested I take them up and back in the coach. They jumped at the chance. Just then a beautiful young police woman came into the pub had a word with the landlord and on her way out stopped to speak to us in a friendly way.

When she got to our table one of the girls introduced her to me and said, "Alan's taking us by coach to the dance on Thursday. Why don't you come with us?" The police woman, Jean, accepted the invitation and told us,"I am on a different route tomorrow so I'll see you on Wednesday." Sure enough on Wednesday she checked in at the pub, spoke to us and left. Thursday arrived and Jean came into the pub looking more lovely than ever in her own clothes. At the hall I had a couple of dances with her and we chatted. When I drove them back home after they were all very merry with drink they began all saying cheerio and goodnight to one another. Jean said to me, "I will be on duty tomorrow and will say goodbye to you when I come in as it's your last night." The next evening I was having a drink with these wonderful friends I had made when in came Jean.

She spoke to the landlord as usual, then beckoned me over. "Would you like to go for a ride?" I thought I might as well - I was only drinking - so I jumped into her police car. Up the road she went and turned into a small lane and then into a narrow track leading into a forest. I wondered what she could be checking up on here, when she stopped the car.

She said, "I wanted to say goodbye to you and thank you for a lovely evening yesterday and to give you something to remember me by when you get home." We started kissing and then made passionate love, in her small Panda police car, Jean in her police uniform. Afterwards she said, "I have got to hurry otherwise people will wonder why I am late making my calls". So she dropped me back at the pub said cheerio, and she was gone.

I went back into the pub and had a last drink with them all. I had a wonderful weekend and will certainly not forget that Friday night with Jean. It was an interview with the police I will always remember.

Very Irregular

Shortly after I was on tour driving a coach with Hampshire County Cricket Club who were playing matches against the Brussels Cricket Club and the British Army team. In the County team were Roy Marshall, Gordon Greenidge, and Butch White who was big built and over six feet tall, towering above me. But everywhere we went he told people I was his brother.

In the match against the army he was batting and I was running drinks out to the players when they needed them as it was a hot day. When Butch called out for one I ran onto the pitch and gave it to him. As he took the drink he handed me his bat and said "You can take my turn." He was, of course only joking, but the colonel who was captain of the Army side said in a very posh voice, "This is all very irregular!" We both collapsed with laughter at the look on his face.

Spanish Adventures

In the mid to late 1960s, I drove many coaches of tourists to Spain and back. On one trip to Spain we had stopped overnight at Laval in France and were on the next leg to Toulouse. As we were approaching Limoges the engine lost power and would scarcely turn over. We were climbing the hill just before we dropped into the town, so I got all the passengers off and asked them to push the coach about 150 yards to the top of the hill. We coasted down into the town.

When we arrived we found everything was closed on a Sunday but we were lucky - we pulled up at a small garage which had a sign "Diesel Specialist" where the owner was still open doing some odd jobs. He said he would get the coach repaired by 3pm the next day and arranged a hotel and two taxis to shuttle the passengers. We had a slap up meal and everybody was happy. Next morning I paid for them all to go to the swimming baths and bought sweets for the children.

When I got to the garage to pick up coach the owner told me it needed a new fuel pump. He had tried everywhere in Europe with no success and I would have to get one from England. I got back to the hotel, told the passengers and said we will get back home on the Saturday instead of Friday so they would have an extra day's holiday. It was more quiet over dinner that night. I phoned Jack Jacobs, the owner, and he went to Ford's at Dagenham, picked up a new pump and put it on the 10 pm car ferry to Calais with instructions for them to put it on the train to Paris where the French equivalent of the Automobile Association would transfer it to a Limoges train. It would arrive at 4 pm and the mechanic said it would only take one hour to fit.

We waited on the platform. The train arrived. No pump. Someone had forgotten to transfer it in Paris. You can imagine by now the customers are getting angry and starting to shout, asking why did I not hire another coach. I explained that he would not be allowed over the border because he would not have a license and there was a 3-mile no-man's-land between the French and Spanish borders. Only a few weeks earlier a British coach had broken down and had hired a French coach but after 20 miles the passengers had refused to go any further.

I then told my people I would get them home on the Sunday so they would have two more days of holiday. The pump arrived on the Wednesday and at 4pm was ready to go. By the time I had got back to the hotel and loaded luggage we departed at six and I drove all through the night and arrived at the camp site at Malgret-de-Mar at 10 am. The people there started coming out of their tents expecting to go home as we took one party down and brought other party home. I used to arrive back in Southampton 8pm Friday evening and leave again on 10 am boat on Saturday.

I told the returning passengers that I would not be starting back until next day because I had to get some sleep. So next morning I left at 6 am and drove straight up to Laval – 18 hours and when we arrived at the hotel it was in darkness. But all the room keys had been left on the desk at reception with a note from Jack, the coach owner, to say that the new coach which I had seen outside was a "top up" and my new passengers would be ready at 8am to go to Spain.

This meant we were back on schedule for both parties. But unfortunately that didn't satisfy my passengers. They had been given two days extra holiday, had been paid to go swimming and even given money to spend yet when they got back home they sent a delegation to demand their money back. Jack offered them £5 off any future trip – remember they had only paid in those days £25 for four nights hotel B&B, all their tents on site with any gas they needed, the cross channel ferry both ways plus the trip out by coach. They refused this offer and contacted the daily papers. When the reporters heard our side of the story did not carry anything about the complaints. The experience could not have been that bad because half of them came again the following year!

Around this time, I was on my way back from Spain with a coach and had just got past Laval in France when I came to a small roundabout. Seeing it was all clear I started to go round it when suddenly a car came from nowhere at speed and I hit him on his front wheel, smashing it in. He got out of his car, shouting and screaming at me, and I could not understand a word he was saying. Luckily there was a French man present who saw the accident it and could speak perfect English. He explained to me that the driver's wife was pregnant and that was why he was in a hurry. He explained it to the French police when they arrived and they let me carry on.

On one of the occasions when we were at Malgret-de-Mar in Spain one of my passengers, a man who was bathing the sea, shouted out and then started sinking. He was pulled from the water and medics were called but he had died. Some thought he had drowned but it was a heart attack. He was with his wife and two children and this was their third day with seven more days to go.

I had to go to the British Embassy in Barcelona to see if they could fly his body home which had to be in a lead coffin and it was not until the day of our departure that I got the message that they could fly him, otherwise I could imagine me putting his body in the boot of the coach to get him home. I tried to look after the rest of the family as best I could on the way home but made a big mistake when we got to Southampton docks. Before all the passengers got off, I got up as I usually did and said "I hope to see you all again and that you had a great holiday", then realized the wife was sat where I was standing. I could have wished the ground would open up and swallow me.

47

When in Malgret-de-Mar I used to take the coach party around to Callea one evening a week where we always visited the same restaurant. I got friendly with the Spanish waitress and found out her mother owned the place. After about six weeks, I asked her if she would like to go out for a meal somewhere different. She agreed and we arranged a time. When I arrived she was waiting for me at the entrance to her café, put her arms around me and gave me a kiss on the cheek. Then she said "Do you want to come in for a drink first?" I said "No let's just go". She asked me to wait a minute, went inside and came out with her mother. At first I thought Mum had come to say goodbye. But then I realized she was coming with us. In those days a lot of mothers in Spain escorted their daughters when they went out with someone. The daughter spoke brilliant English but the mother could not speak a word so it was a very strained evening. I never used her restaurant again.

End of Season

At the end of the summer season, driving backwards and forwards to Spain, the hotels, bars and clubs we used to stop at for our breaks gave us drivers gifts as a thank you – usually a bottle of something. When I came back from the last trip of the summer and pulled into the terminal at Southampton, a customs officer took all the passengers off as usual and told them to take their cases to the tables for inspection. He then went through the coach with a fine tooth comb looking for contraband. When he got to the front seat, he found all the things I was bringing back – brandy, gin, scotch, Bacardi and lots of cigarettes. Half of these were the gifts I'd received and half were drink I'd bought. I explained it was my last trip this summer season and that they were gifts. "I know it's not legal," I told him, "So if you want to take them away from me, you can." He decided my reason for having them was legitimate, then got off the coach and looked through the passengers' luggage. He said to me, "Why didn't you ask some of your passengers to take stuff as they do not have their full duty allowance?" I replied that I couldn't do anything like that as it would be illegal.

A Rescue Mission

Six months after finishing with Jacobs Coaches, in 1968, I was out of work and sitting in my bedsit when there was a knock on the door. I found Jack standing there. He said "I was wondering if you would go to Spain to collect a coach and bring the passengers home?" It was a Friday so I told him, "Yes, as long as on Monday you go to the civic centre and pick up the keys to a council flat they have given me and that I'm due to collect."

On Monday I flew from Heathrow to Barcelona and then on by train to Malgret-de-Mar. On the way I wondered why there was no driver there to bring the coach back. Perhaps he was taken ill? Jack had not told me. But when I arrived I soon found out the true story.

Rod Weber used to drive taxis but did a bit of part time coach work and Jack knew he would be stuck for a driver on this trip so had asked him some weeks before. In the next couple of weeks, Rod chatted up an escort who worked for Summerfields. He asked her "Are you going on holiday?" She replied that she couldn't afford a holiday with a young daughter. Rod said, "Would you like to go to Spain – it won't cost you anything. I can get you on the coach and boat free." So, of course, she said yes. At the first hotel stop in France, he gave out the room keys to the passengers and she went up to her room. A few minutes later her bedroom door opened and in walked Rod. She said, "What do you want?" To which he replied, "I'm sleeping here tonight."

She told him "no" and kicked him out. The second night the same thing happened. By the time they reached Spain at lunchtime she had made friends with other people and had arranged to go out in the evening with them. Rod had told the people on the coach that she was his wife and he was now embarrassed as she was telling everybody he was not her husband.

He left them all there and flew home. He walked into the coach office and gave Jack the coach keys.

In the two days I was in Spain before we returned home I was introduced to the woman concerned, Although I recognized her I had never spoken to her before and she said she disliked his attitude of taking for granted that she would sleep with him. I felt

49

she was a bit naïve if she expected a holiday for nothing. It was Rod's fault as he should have said in the first place that if she came she would have to sleep with him. Then she could have straightened him out right from the start.

European Cup

I was still driving coaches for Jacobs in 1968 when we had the European Cup final at Wembley between Manchester United and Benfica of Portugal.

We had two coaches picking up passengers at Southampton Airport from Guernsey to go to the Derby at Epsom and then onto the European Cup Final at Wembley. After leaving Epsom, we both and started to make our way to our next destination but after about two miles I lost the other coach who got held up in traffic. So I made my way towards London and picked up the South Circular, then onto the North Circular, then turned left for Harrow and up to Wembley Way.

The coaches were supposed to go over Roundabout Road then turn right the other side of the ice rink onto the coach park but I decided that as it was getting near to the kick off time I would turn right at Roundabout Road and go down Wembley Way. I was stopped by a security guard who said "Where do you think you are going?" I pointed to my passengers and said "Guernsey and French FA Officials," He said, "carry on." As I got to the end of the road near the stadium I was stopped again and told the same story. This time the official said, "Where is your pass? You should have it on your windscreen." I said, "we broke down and when we changed coaches I forgot to take it with me."

He gave me the OK and said, "Go and park by those coaches over there." Four motors were parked by the players' entrance so I pulled alongside them and told my passengers to come back straight after the match finished. The organiser Les Delamare had got all his tickets from Benfica FC because on the island - which employed a lot of Portuguese people - they had a football team. I locked the coach up and was wondering how I could get in to see the match when a smart gentleman in a suit who was talking to the four drivers there said to me, "Did they give you your ticket?" I said "No" and he pulled a ticket out of his pocket and handed it to me. I had no idea who he thought I was but I found out a few minutes later. When I went into the stadium I found I was sat with all the players' wives and families.

As I arrived the players were coming out onto the pitch and families started shouting out "Hello Matt" (Busby),"Hello Nobby" (Stiles), "Hello Bobby" (Charlton) in their northern accents so I joined in shouting, trying to sound as northern as possible..

It was a great match which Man U won in extra time. Afterwards I went straight back to the coach and when all my passengers were on board headed back up Wembley Way. But when I tried to join the main road with my indicator signalling left, a policeman stopped me and said, "You have got go right for the North." I said "Guernsey and French FA Officials - we have got a plane being held up at Heathrow for us." He said, "wait a minute", and he spoke to a police motorcyclist on the other side of the road. Then he told me, "Follow him."

So we had a police escort, all the traffic moved over and we flew past them. Then he went ahead of us and stopped all the traffic on the North Circular and as we swung right onto it, gave us a wave and I waved back. I was relieved he was not going to give us an escort all the way to Heathrow airport because we were going in the other direction. I drove up to Hanger Lane then turned left onto the A40 and into London where we were stopping the night in a hotel in Bayswater.

It was 11.25 pm so we checked our bags in our rooms and went down to Soho and got back about 3 am. We then learned that the other coach did not arrived there until 1.30 but I was not surprised as there must have been 200 coaches in the Wembley coach park and he was made to turn right and pick up the north circular further up then double back down to London.

Twenty years later I met Les Delamare, the organiser again, because we belong to the SKAL Club. We used to meet up at functions all over the country and he often came back my house to stay with his wife, Val. But everywhere he went he told people about me and our trip to Wembley.

Dumb Waiter

The bad luck fairy was still following me around. As well as driving coaches I was also still working at the Carousel Night Club. Part of my job was to take the empty crates from the bar and load them on to the dumb waiter to go down to the cellar. I was on my second load and had put five crates on then pressed the button but I did not hear it go down so I opened the shutter and found it was still stuck there. I then noticed that one crate was caught up on the side so I pushed it to get it fully on and the lift suddenly dropped and caught both my wrists. I was on tip toe, falling forwards and my back was hurting, so I began shouting as loud as I could. The night club was empty but I knew there was still someone in the kitchen below. At last they heard me and called the ambulance and fire brigade who used a crowbar to prise the lift up to get my hands out but they then withdrew the bar and the lift crashed down to the cellar – when it had stuck at the top the cable had still unwound as though it had gone down. I was taken to hospital where they x–rayed my wrists. I was shaken up but realized that I had been very lucky - if I had pulled my hands back quicker the lift could have caught my fingers and chopped them off. That night the local paper, The Echo carried a story with the headline "Man trapped in lift" which made it sound worse than it was.

My next job was different again. I worked for the British Automatic Company from Bristol driving a company van and visiting railway stations around Hampshire filling the sweet machine up and collecting the money. I also visited shops that had children's rides as well as emptying cash from all the telescopes along the coast at Southsea and Bournemouth and the weighing machines. I also emptied the "one arm bandit" gambling machines on the British Rail ferry from Weymouth. I must have been too good at this job. It was the only round making money, so BAC sold it off to another company, and I got laid off.

From one-arm bandits I went in 1969 into the bakery business as area manager for Wilkins the bakers from Bournemouth. My job was to look after 12 shops from Fareham, Gosport and through to Southampton. I also had to employ the staff, make sure they were ordering enough cakes and bread and do a stocktake of each shop every 12 weeks.

One day I was stocktaking one of our shops at Fareham and found some items missing. I called the manageress in and asked her where they were. She denied having taken them. I told her that if she admitted the theft I would not call the police in. She would still get the sack but her friends and staff will not know about it. She refused the offer so I called the police. They searched her house and found the missing items. Two days later I was called to a meeting with our sales manager who told me he had to dismiss me because I should have taken a stock check before and it was the company's policy not to call in the police. I protested that not calling the police provided no deterrent but it was of no avail. I had done nothing wrong as I had stocktaken on time, but still carried the can for the theft that I had uncovered and dealt with.

Eye to Eye

It's odd how even after 50 years a single moment and a single glance can stay in your memory. One evening in 1969 I was in the Sillhouette night club sat at the bar. Three spaces away from me was a lovely girl, by herself. I smiled at her, she smiled at me and I invited her to join me for a drink. She said, "You have talking eyes and I can read what you want but you are going to be unlucky tonight because my boy friend will be here in a minute." A minute or two later he arrived and that was that. I had been told twice before about my eyes. So I had another drink, alone, and went home. You can't win all the time.

the transatlantics

Above: A publicity photo for the group I managed – The Transatlantics, 1964. **Below Left:** Crewing aboard Viking II, 1965. **Below Right:** Looking handsome on land, the same year.

Serving drinks in the Bar Restaurant of The Carousel night club, in Southampton, 1965.

Floor manager at the Top Hat, Ballroom in Southampton, in 1966.

One of the Big Beat dances I promoted at Southampton Guildhall.

Chapter 4
1970s - Marriage to Patsy

The 1970s started out with me still working at night clubs around Southampton and living the bachelor existence. But it wasn't long before that was going to change dramatically – but I'm getting ahead of myself. Life for a single young man in the 1970s could be quite colourful.

One night around 1971 we had a function at the Top Hat Ballroom. It was a "men only" night with a meal and some female entertainment of a revealing kind. Bob Fagan was the first club owner in Britain to put on evenings of this kind and the daily newspapers used to write about us. There were traditional strip clubs in places like Soho, but in our club you had to be a member and we did things on a grand scale - with 150 men members attending.

After the meal was finished and the waitresses had cleared everything away I sent them downstairs and put a screen up across the top of the stairs so no-one could come up and spy on the act to come. I then went to the dressing room to tell the girls to start their act. The first one was halfway through her act when there was an almighty bang as the screen fell over to disclose four waitresses all bent over who had been peering through slits in the screen, like a scene from a stage comedy. They dived back down the stairs to the kitchen. The stripper screamed and ran back to the dressing room so I picked up her garments and went "back stage" to the dressing room to apologise. It seemed to me strange that the ladies we engaged felt able to strip in front of all those men but got upset at other women looking at them.

The strippers we hired were well able to take care of themselves if the customers got out of hand. On another men-only night the artist was doing her act in the middle of the floor when one silly young man who had had too much to drink threw a full glass of beer over her. She carried on until she got to the table where the lad who threw it was sitting, sat on the lap of a person opposite and then, in a second, picked his pint of beer up and emptied it all over him. He was angry but his mates forced him back in his seat told him, "You deserved that."

After each act I would collect the discarded clothes and take them into the dressing room where I would sit and chat to the girls. I became such a familiar face that they would not take any notice of me. When they had all finished their acts, I would take them downstairs to the Night Club where their husbands were waiting to buy them a drink. I could not understand how a man would allow his partner or wife to perform as they did. I would certainly have not.

I continued to work at the Carousel Night Club, part-time during the Summer and full-time in the Winter. There were, of course many attractive young women who worked at the club. Among them was one particularly attractive girl called Patsy. I did sometimes date girls from the club but Patsy evidently didn't take much of a shine to me and I didn't take much of a shine to her. Until one night, on New Year's Eve, we found ourselves coming down in the lift, just the two of us, and I suddenly on impulse said, "Give us a New Year's kiss, Patsy." And to my surprise, she did. That was the start of 46 years together. When we were to get married a year later all the staff told her, "It will never last" and told her stories about my past. But luckily they didn't put her off. Somehow we were made for each other and we stayed together.

Rabbit out of a hat

I don't know if it was some kind of good omen but one night after I left Patsy and was driving home, I found a large white rabbit sitting in the middle of the road. I stopped the car and walked round to him and picked him up. He was so tame he didn't resist and I took him home with me. I advertised him but got no replies. I wasn't able to keep him and I knew Bill Summerfield kept rabbits, so I offered him to Bill who was pleased to take him. But when I saw Bill a week later and asked after the white rabbit, he was angry as the rabbit had torn his hutch to bits. I don't think he had ever been locked away before because he was so friendly. I wondered if he had escaped from a magician.

Like me, Patsy had been married before. She had three children. After Patsy and I were married it was difficult to begin with because I was the strange man who moved into their house to live instead of their dad, and was trying my hardest to be a father to Kim who was nearly 14 years, Dale 12 years and Stuart five and a half. Understandably, they did not like this strange new man at all.

With hindsight it's easy to see we should have gone out with the kids first, and I should have got to know them better before we married, so they had a chance to get used to me and find out I was only human. I expect many men and women have been in the same position as I was and will understand the difficulty it creates in making a whole new set of relationships, all at once.

As time went on our relations got much better although it was hardest for Kim, the oldest. I'm happy to say that was to change a few years later when she got married. The reception was held at the hall behind the church so there was no alcohol and I had got a friend of mine to do the buffet as he was an excellent chef and it was only going to cost £150 – what a difference to today's massive wedding bills. Kim's dad, Tony, said he would go halves with me but somehow never got round to it. It was about four months later I got home from work and Patsy said, "We are going up our friends' house for dinner". I could not believe it when we arrived and Kim opened the door, put her arms round me and said, "I'm sorry for the way I have been to you." That hug meant everything to me. Dale was also coming round to me, and then he got married too, and of course, marriage usually brings families closer together. Stuart was always just himself and we always seemed to get along just fine.

Jewellery Salesman

Having become a married man, I needed a steady job, so I went to the Labour Exchange to see what they could offer me. At that stage I didn't have any real idea what I wanted to do, except that I wanted regular work and a decent wage. Three weeks later they sent for me and arranged for me to attend an interview that they thought I may be interested in. There were about 20 of us in the room and the gentleman who interviewed us introduced himself as Mr Colley from James Keir Jewellers in Cardiff. The jewellers were looking for an area sales rep for the Hampshire area. It was not cold selling door to door. Instead the rep would go out with the Provident collector on his rounds The Provident man would introduce the rep to their regular customers.

Perhaps I should explain that Provident was a company that issued vouchers so you could go to certain shops on their list to buy furniture and other household items. Then the buyer would pay back the sum owed in weekly instalments. It was an early form of Hire-Purchase.

After he had described the job to us, he asked if we had any questions. No-one else asked anything but I wanted to know how many weeks holiday you got, what were the chances of promotion and so on. He then asked "Who wants the job?" Four of us put up our hands. He pointed to me and said, "I will see you first," and asked the others to wait outside. I assumed that he liked the fact that I had asked questions.

We spoke for a few minutes and he told me, "The job's yours. "Fill out this bond form. I need this because you will be carrying a case with about £5,000 worth of jewellery."

The wages were £20 per week plus a £20 car allowance and commission on sales. I am a soft seller and when the Provident rep took me to a customer I would take the trays out of the case for her to look at and let her take her time. I never pushed them to buy but when they picked something up or was looking at a piece I would say that will only cost you – say – £1 a week and it was going to cost them over two years £40 more than the purchase price.

The company put up prizes for the most sales and on one occasion the target was £2000 sales in a week. I was down in Portsmouth and the rep took me to what she said was her best customer. The customer started picking stuff up and putting it to one side and it came to about £1,100. I started to pack up the rest of my jewellery and she said, "Keep it out, my sister will be here in a minute." When I left the house I had taken £1,850 on a Monday morning. I thought I was sure to win the prize, but the rest of the week I did not take a penny. So I went and saw the manager and told him I had three call-backs to do on that Friday evening – I might still make it. As it was I got another £500 sales, and easily won the prize.

I had been with the company for a year when I was promoted to sales manager, Southern England with 12 reps under me. My wages were increased to £30 per week plus £30 car allowance and commission of 5% rising to 7.5% and then 10% according to sales figures plus all hotel expenses paid. After another nine months I was promoted again to sales manager of the UK. I was heading for the top - but two months later the sales director left, for reasons I never learned, and the chief accountant took over.

I then had messages left at the hotel asking me to I contact Cardiff and I had that feeling I was going to get the sack so I ignored the messages for four days. When I finally got in contact with head office they said they wanted to see me and to bring my bag with me which I carried in case any of my now 24 reps wanted any of the items. It was as I feared. There had been some kind of revolution at the top and I was no longer wanted.

After getting the sack I went to the labour exchange and they advised me to take them to a tribunal for unfair dismissal and redundancy as I had been with them for 2 years and 2 months. The case was heard at Bristol. The company was losing the case and after lunch admitted redundancy. I spoke to one of the panel after and he told me if I had just taken them for unfair dismissal I would have got £30,000 – equivalent to one year's salary - instead of just £80. I blame the labour exchange for the bad advice they gave me.

Job Hunting Again

Despite the bad advice, I went back to the labour exchange to find another job. My wages were so high I had to go to the executive office the other side of the road to the ordinary office. The woman I spoke to gave me a long form to fill out with lots of questions. I looked at them – what university had I gone to? Which college? How many A Levels I had? I just crossed them all out and signed it. When the woman saw the blank form, she said, "How did you get the jobs you had?" I said, "From the labour exchange." She said, "I will not be able to get you a job where you will be earning more than the prime minister." I had left school with nothing – bottom of English and science but top in maths.

Three weeks went by and then they sent for me, as they had a job I may be interested in for a salesman for Hobarts who supplied large dishwashers and other machines for ships, hotels and factories. I went for the interview and got the job. But later, in the evening, started to have second thoughts. I said to Patsy, "I don't know whether I really want the job. I can't see myself sitting with company directors to sell them the product." So I sent them a letter saying I had taken another position. Two and a half weeks later I got my first wage packet from them. I did not send it back because I thought they should have been more efficient for a large company!

I kept looking for something that was more "me" and got a job at Rowe and company (no relation) who were vegetable merchants. I used to deliver to local schools three days a week as well as other sites in Hampshire. I stayed there six months. At the same time I continued working in nightclubs in Southampton as a barman part time and a waiter in the Astor Club, The Carol Club, The Key Club, The Carousel Club and The Rainbow Club.

During the same period I was also working part time and self-employed between jobs as a coach driver for Colosseum Coaches, in West End, Easson's Coaches, at Woolston, Watson's Coaches, of St Denys, Trev's Travel, in Fairoak, Anglia Coaches, in Lowford and Princess Summerbee, in West End.

Driving was never boring and even the most ordinary trip could turn into something to look back on and laugh about. Like the time I had been out all day on a coach trip for Colisseum Coaches and I did not have a full load so when a couple got on with a baby in a carry cot I told them, "You can put it on the back seat as it's not being used." On the way back I didn't take much notice as people got off at their various stops and when I'd finished the route, I pulled into the yard and parked the coach. I was just locking it up when I heard a cry, looked inside and found the baby was still on the back seat. Moments later a car came tearing into the yard and the couple got out, asking, "Where is our baby?" They had got off and forgotten about the baby.

In 1974, I joined the Provident Company as a collector calling on people to collect money for vouchers they had bought on credit to use in local shops. This was the job I had worked together with as a jewellery salesman, although now I was no longer the second fiddle. I was given a round for Wednesday, Thursday, Friday and Saturday morning. I soon got rid of the bad payers and asked a few people if they minded me calling up to 10:30 at night. In this way I got my round to Thursday from 5 pm, Friday from 2 pm and no Saturdays and was earning £90 a week. This gave me time to do part time coach driving.

The Wrong Way

One of the coach tours I did in 1975 was a trip to Holland. It was a two-driver trip which I did with my colleague Tony and we stayed about 20 miles north of Amsterdam. On the last day we left the hotel and as Tony was driving I went back to check with the passengers and make sure they had a good time. I spent some time talking and did not pay much attention to the route we were taking. By the time I took a good look out of the window, expecting to see the buildings of Amsterdam, I could see we must have taken a wrong turning. I went up to the front of the coach to ask Tony where he was heading when a turn-off came in sight and I realised we were heading north and not south. It was another 20 miles before we could turn round and by the time we got back to Amsterdam we had lost one and a half hours. I knew we would never make the hovercraft from Calais across the channel so I decided we would instead get a boat from Ostend.

I pulled into the Ostend checkpoint and explained that I had phoned Calais and told them we would not make the crossing so they had said then I had better come here. The ferry official looked at me oddly and said, "That's strange," and laughed. "The hovercraft is not running and has been on shore for the last three days because of the weather."

Sometimes you get found out – and I felt a bit of a fool for making up a story. But he kindly let us on a ferry sailing in an hour.

A Place I'll Never Forget

Most people have in their life one memory they will never forget. The memory which always stays on my mind was a coach trip in 1975, coming back from Bavaria when we stopped at the Dachau concentration camp.

In those days, there were no organised tours or museum. The camp had simply been deserted and left pretty much as it had been 30 years earlier, a very lonely and eerie place. The passengers got off the coach and started walking towards the gate where all the women, Patsy included, turned round and walked or ran back to the coach, with tears in their eyes. I cannot explain how I really felt. It was such an eerie sensation, so quiet, and a horrible smell of decay, with no sign of wild life. The rest of us went in and looked at the gas chambers and the places the Jews were held prisoner and then, at the end of the camp against the boundary fence, we stood for a minute before a memorial to all the people that had perished there. Suddenly we saw a flock of birds flying towards us and turned away at the last moment. It was as if they wanted to fly over the camp site but would not cross the wire fence – as though they could feel that something was wrong.

As I stood there, I made a silent wish that all teenagers and youngsters from 17 to 21 should go to that place to get some idea of what went on in the camp and try to imagine the horrors that the Jews suffered, in the hope their generation will make sure this kind of thing never happens again to human society.

The shadow of the Nazis figured elsewhere on our holiday travels that year. We were on a coach holiday to Konisia in the Bavarian Alps and we were staying at a hotel by a lake above which was the eagle's nest where Hitler used to spend time. On one day we decided to hire a rowing boat and go round the lake and when we wanted a break we would pull into the side get out the glasses and have a drink of Scotch and the spring water coming down the side of the mountain. There was Mike and his daughter Paula and me and Patsy. It was on the way back that we saw the passenger ferry bearing down on us, so we had to row like mad to get out of its way. When we got back to the hotel we decided to go for a sauna but when we walked in with just our bathing trunks on we found all the Swedish and German men and women were sat there naked and they stared giggling at us. We felt so embarrassed. Patsy said she would come on down and join us later. She came in and went to sit down when she saw all the naked people she gave one shriek and dived outside again. We laughed about it later.

Our Own Company

One afternoon in 1976, a chance encounter with an old friend turned out to be a life-changing moment for me and for Patsy. I was walking by Summerfield Hire Services in Aldermoor, a place I knew well as I had driven coaches for Bill Summerfield many times. Bill saw me passing by and came out to speak to me.

To my surprise he said, "Do you know anyone who wants to buy my business?" He had three mini buses plus a taxi. He said he wanted £20,000 for the whole concern. Bill had to get out of the coaching business because he was a chronic asthma sufferer and the doctors had warned him the work could kill him if he did not quit. So, I went home and talked it over with Patsy. We didn't have £20,000 or anything like that that sum. But Bill was desperate to quit and we were attracted to the idea of owning our own coaching business.

I told Bill that I could offer £10,000. He grumbled but accepted my offer. I had agreed to buy the business for £10,000 but I had no money, so I approached the local banks and finance companies. They all turned me down as I had no deposit. So I went back to Bill Summerfield and agreed to pay him £5,000 and £5,000 over two years. I then went to the Midland Bank and they said if I put the £5,000 deposit down they would match it and I could then pay the £10,000 I had agreed.

I went to see Brian Stoner, a friend of mine who owned a car rental business and asked him to give me £5,000. He said all his capital was tied up in his cars. But I said, "If you make a cheque out for five thousand pounds, the bank will give me an account and cheque book and I will come straight back here and give you a cheque for £5,000 to pay into your bank. So it will only be on paper and no money will have changed hands."

This we duly did and I took over the business. Four weeks later I went into the bank and the young bank manager saw me and invited me into his office. He said, "I want you to explain to me why you did not pay Mr Summerfield the £10,000 as we agreed and why £5,000 went to a company named Stoner Self Drive?"

I said I had agreed to pay the £5,000 over two years and in addition I was involved with the other company and realized that unless I gave them back the money they had lent me, they would be in financial trouble. He asked me how things were going and I explained they were not going well as Patsy was in hospital and I was having to do two jobs to make ends meet.

I got up to leave and as I got to the door he said, "You are a very good liar, Mr Rowe". But I had not lied – I had simply not told him the whole truth, otherwise I would not have been loaned the money. Several years later, by which time Summerfields was very successful, I received a phone call from him, inviting me to lunch. He had been in the Channel Islands for some time and had just returned. Over lunch he told me that the loan he had made to me was his first – and it had caused him sleepless nights and nightmares.

So Patsy and I found ourselves the owners of Summerfields Coaches and we took over the business on 1st May 1976. I can be precise about the date because our first job was to take all the minibuses up to Wembley Stadium where the Saints – Southampton Football Club – beat Manchester United in the FA Cup Final. We were up and running and off to a great start but it was very far from plain sailing.

Two months after we took over Patsy had to be admitted to Lord Mayor Treloar Hospital at Alton for a spinal fusion and was there for eight weeks. At the same time I was still doing my Provident job to make ends meet and visiting Patsy so it was very hard going to start with, with me working 16 hours a day seven days a week. Luckily, our daughter Kim used to help out on Saturday mornings for a couple of years.

The office was a small shed on council land and was on a lease. After the first nine months we got rid of it and put a

Portakabin in its place. We also got rid of the taxi to concentrate on building the coach side up.

Patsy was a director and Secretary of the company whose name we had officially changed to Summerfield Coaches. By 1984 we had built the company up so we had 20 and 35 seaters and seven minibuses in the fleet. We then approached the council for land on the opposite side of the road to build a coach compound and move our Portakabin there as a drivers' room. They not only agreed to this but also to our building two shops with offices above where our Portakabin now stood. It was all completed and officially opened by the Mayor of Southampton, Councillor Mrs D Brown on the 8th May 1984. From then on we gradually increased the fleet to include 49 and 53 seaters and by 1990 had a fleet of 12 vehicles – three with 53 seats, two at 49, two at 35, two at 20, one at16, two at 12 seats.

But I'm getting a bit ahead of myself and this de luxe vehicle fleet still lay in the future, after half a dozen years of hard graft.

On the Town

In 1977, an agent from a shipping company phoned to book a 20 seater to take about 16 foreign seamen off a boat to go on a night on the town. I went and picked them up and as soon as they were all on board they said "Sex. Girls. You take us." The customer is always right so I took them to Derby Road which was the red light district in Southampton. I stopped the coach and explained to the seaman that this was the place they were looking for. I told them, "When you are finished I will be parked at the end of the road." When they all got back they were exchanging notes about the girls they had met. I then took them to a night club in St Mary's Street, parked up and went in with them. A few minutes later two CID detectives I recognized came into the club. They came straight over to me and said "The next time we catch you doing what you did in Derby Road we will book you."

It was never easy finding good drivers. One day I was advertising for a coach driver who had to have continental experience as I had a tour coach going out on the Friday and so far had no luck finding someone to drive it. The phone rang on Monday morning and a woman's voice asked me if she could send her boy friend up for an interview. I told her to send him up as soon as possible and she promised to get him there tomorrow. She told me he had been bringing coaches up from Spain and changing over halfway through France then returning to Spain, and this was exactly what I was looking for.

I interviewed the young man, Don, and took him on to start the tour on Friday. When I got home that evening Patsy said, "Did you take him on?" When I said I had she asked, "What was he like?"

I said he was OK as far as driving was concerned but I could not understand a word he said. He was a proper Geordie from Newcastle. He was staying with his girlfriend's mother and father. She had met him on holiday and it often doesn't work out with people living so far apart but they later got married and Patsy and me were invited to the wedding festivities in the evening. They then bought their own house and Don told me later that if I had not taken him on he would never have got married or had his own home because in Newcastle they only got a third of the wages that I was paying him. Don turned out one of the best drivers I ever employed. He got on with people and his coach always spotlessly clean – you could eat your food off the floor inside. I still see him from time to time.

Caravan Holiday

In 1978 we were doing well enough for me to buy a Royal caravan. I had done it all up and we were going to take it on holiday with us to the Snowdonia area along with our friends Derek and Doreen who were bringing their caravan. What we didn't know was that my traffic jinx was waiting for us. We set off and were on the M5 heading towards the M6, I was leading and was just coming down an incline when I felt something pulling the car from the inside lane to the middle lane and then to the outside lane. My friends could see there was something wrong so Derek pulled his caravan so it straddled the first two lanes to stop other cars from crashing into me. By this time I was seriously worried about going into the central barrier so I swung the steering wheel around to avoid it. The caravan overturned and the next thing I knew we were sliding down the motorway with the car still hitched up facing back from where we had come.

It all happened so quickly. And there, coming towards me was a coach on the outside lane. Luckily, it stopped before it hit me. Then out from the coach poured a small army of soldiers. They got round the caravan and lifted it back upright and I dragged it to the hard shoulder. A few minutes later the police arrived and were amazed the motorway was clear with no holdups as they had only got the message of a traffic accident a few minutes earlier when it was picked up by the TV cameras. They got a breakdown recovery lorry to load it up to take away. We were going to go home but our friends said we could sleep in their awning and both the boys could sleep in their car so we carried on.

There was an unexpected sequel about four months later when I got a phone call from a man who asked me if I had the two missing cushions from the caravan I had smashed up. There was a lot of damage, with all of one side smashed in, plus the back was hanging off but he had just bought it to go touring as someone had put it back together. The reason for the crash was that the stub axle on the offside wheel had gone.

New Ventures

Despite adventures like this, the coach business continued to grow so we decided to expand by opening a couple of shops in the new Summerfield building we had erected. One we decided to turn into a video shop called Video Rowe with videos and some electrical items like TV, wireless, recorders and other electrical goods. The idea was a good one but it didn't work out for the area we were in so we dropped the electrical side and concentrated on video rentals. My son Dale managed the shop for us and made such a great success of it that 18 months later we opened another shop in Townhill Park. But it was not doing well so he closed it after six months. Dale was getting bored after doing the job for three years and left. I did not blame him because there was a lot of sitting around when business was slack. Patsy and I kept it going for another couple of months then closed it. We then rented the entire shop out.

The second shop we decided to open was a travel agency. With the help of John from Tour South who were renting office space from us for their own tourism business we started up and called it Patala Travel. After four months we realised it was not going to succeed in that area and we were losing money so we let a more experienced company take it over who already had three shops, Watson's Travel. But after about another four months they closed down and we then rented that shop out as well.

I have no regrets about trying these new ventures – after all if you don't even try you'll never know whether or not you can succeed. It's a bit like giving up before you've even started. So we concentrated again on travel and tourism centred around coaching and as the 1980s dawned, this became a golden age for a coaching company like ours.

Top left*: At the wheel, 1965,* ***Top right****: Girona, Spain, 1967,*

Middle left: *1967,* ***Middle right****: France 1968,*

Bottom lef: *Coach breakdown, France 1967. The passengers kindly helped get the coach over the hill and into town!*

Chapter 5
1980s - Tour Operator

There were 26 coach operators in the Association of Southampton and District Coach Operators when I was elected Chairman in 1979, a position I held for two years. I realized straight away that I had to change how operators felt about one another as some did not even talk to one another and, for example, would not help out a fellow operator if they had a breakdown or needed a coach for extra work. I arranged a couple of promotions, one to France and one to Denmark. I got hold of the tourist boards in those countries and the ferry companies for a free crossing so it did not cost us much but it meant all the operators were together on the coach as well as in the bars in the hotels. As I hoped, they all found that "the bloke up the road" was not as bad as they thought and four of us became firm friends, going out with our wives to celebrate everybody's birthday I'm pleased to say that today all operators will help one another out. The coach sales reps will tell you we are the only association in the country like it, and unfortunately many of the other associations are still like we were at the start.

At the beginning of the 1980s, I became chairman of the Southampton Hotels Association. We worked together with the city's tourism department to increase the popularity of Southampton as a tourist destination. One of the first things I realized was that you could not sell Southampton by itself but needed the attractions from the surrounding area to draw people in, so I persuaded them to change the name to South Hampshire Tourism Group. This meant we attracted new members like Paultons Park, Beaulieu Motor Museum, Marwell Zoo amongst other attractions as well as more hotels from the New Forest and surrounding areas. We then produced our own brochure to circulate at travel and holiday fairs.

I remember attending a public meeting one day at the civic centre where the subject under discussion was building a monorail around Southampton city centre and going down as far as the town quay. I told the meeting that they were not being ambitious enough and they should consider extending it to Totton and Eastleigh Airport. Sadly, this tourist idea from the 1980s never got off the ground. I think this was a big missed opportunity because as well as being a great tourist attraction it would also have cut car pollution because they could have built car parks at the furthest points so people would not bring cars into the city centre. An opportunity missed.

Missing Man

In 1982 I took a coach party from a Women's Guild on a trip to Longleat. There were 46 passengers, all of course women but there was also one man - the organiser's husband. He sat at the back of the coach on his own. When the tour of Longleat was finished they all got back on the coach. I was in the driver's seat reading a book so had not taken much notice as they got on. The organiser who sat at the front said, "OK driver - you can go."

We stopped at Salisbury for tea before returning to Southampton. All the ladies got off the coach except the organiser who was waiting for her husband. Then she said to me, "Where is he? You must have left him behind." I said, "But you told me to leave. You will have to go back for him. I can't do that." How he got home I do not know because there are no buses or trains from Longleat and I dare not think what happened to him when he got home. He might have preferred staying with the lions at Longleat to facing what awaited him.

SKAL!

It was towards the end of the 1970s that I first joined an organisation that was to become important in our lives over the next four decades – SKAL – so I had better explain just what it is. SKAL (pronounced Skol) is the Scandinavian drinking toast, their word for "cheers" or "bottoms up". It's an international business organisation for the managers and owners of companies in the travel and tourism business – airlines, shipping lines, coach operators, hotels, travel agents, attractions – anyone in the tourism field.

The organisation has regional clubs all over the UK where regular functions and meetings are held and, of course - being international – events all over the world. We members refer to each other as "Skalleagues" rather than colleagues!

I joined SKAL in 1979 and had the honour to be elected President of the Southampton club in 1985, a role I carried out for two years and had a hard act to follow in my predecessor, Peter Osborne. Patsy and I used to attend SKAL functions at other clubs around the country and the highlight of each year was the President's dinner and dance. Over the coming years, we also attended many international events, as I shall relate.

One of our most memorable Skal International trips was to Israel in 1983. We were taken out to the Dead Sea in the afternoon for a swim but the joke is that it's almost impossible to swim. Every time you get into the water you are pushed up because of the amount of salt in the water and I have got pictures of us sat on the sea reading a paper. In the Bible Jesus walks on water but was he able to because of the salt? It makes you wonder.

In the evening we were given robes and headwear for a Bedouin banquet on the beach and on the other side of the water we could see the flashes of bombs going off in the sky and the boom of guns – the contrast could not have been greater and it was an experience I'll never forget.

After the Israel conference a party of us travelled on to Egypt and our coach had an army escort across the desert. After we had gone through the checkpoint into Egypt we drove along a modern four-lane highway going into Cairo. But there were ancient sights as well as modern - all the traffic was stopped to let a young Arab boy lead his flock of sheep across the road.

The next day four of us went to see the pyramids and there were camels you could have a ride on – if you paid. Wilhelmina wanted to have a go so Eric had to pay one dollar. She got on the camel, which rose to its feet, then galloped off in the distance. Eric said, "Bring her back!" The camel man replied, "Yes sir - for another one dollar." The camel came back but would not sit down to let her get off, so he had to give another dollar to get the camel master to lower the camel. Those camels were obviously well-trained in making money.

We went inside one of the pyramids up very steep steps and when we got to the top entered a chamber where the king or queen was buried. It made me wonder how they could have built these amazing structures all those thousands of years ago.

We then travelled down to Luxor and saw women washing their clothes on the rocks by the banks of the Nile. Everywhere you looked were scenes from ancient history and memories of the Bible times we had read about when we were young.

In 1984 our SKAL International trip was one of the most memorable ever. We went to Las Vegas and we flew there from Los Angeles against very strong headwinds. Most planes were not flying but ours was and I thought we could crash. Even when we landed the winds were so strong the steps down from the plane kept moving and the air hostesses had to help us from the plane to the steps. The winds kept up as our limousine drove us to Caesar's Palace and the tumbleweed was rolling down the streets like in a western film. Even when we got inside at last we found that sand was coming through the air conditioning.

We went to the reception desk on arrival and asked for our rooms. The receptionist asked us, "What room would you like?" The rooms hadn't already been allocated as I assumed and we weren't sure what to ask for when the receptionist said, "I will give you the fantasy suite." She gave us keys and directed us to, "Go through the casino until you come to Joe Louis' statue and take the lift to your floor and the porter will be waiting there with your luggage."

When the porter opened the door and we went inside we were astounded – I had never seen a room like it in my life. It was huge, with a three piece suite, a dining room table and chairs, a king sized bed with see-through drapes around it, two wash basins and the largest circular bath I had ever seen but only but only about a foot deep. The only thing not in the room was the toilet and this had a TV monitor so you could watch betting in the casino and a telephone in case you wanted to put a bet on while answering a call of nature.

We decided to have a bath but the bath was so big that after half an hour the water would not even cover Patsy's and my legs, so in future we decided we would take a shower. That night we got into bed and I noticed the whole ceiling above was covered in mirrors. I said to Patsy, It's OK until you hear a whirring sound – that's when they are filming you. No wonder they called it the fantasy suite.

On one evening of our visit the SKAL club had arranged for us to go to Circus Circus but they were running out of tickets and asked if anyone would like to go and see Dean Martin instead. He was Patsy's favourite artist and his song "Gentle on my mind" the one she liked best so we volunteered. When we got there we found they had placed us on a table right against the stage so we had our meal and then sat back and took in all Dean had to offer. Patsy was over the moon at seeing her favourite singer up so close.

Of course, you can't go to Las Vegas and not gamble. We had saved up £80 to spend and said when it was gone that would be the end. And we won small amounts over the five days we were there but, as usually happens, lost it again. On the final night a farewell banquet was held in the Metropole Hotel opposite ours. So we allowed half an hour to get from our room, through the casino, across the walkway through the second casino in the Metropole and into the hall. It was so far we only just made it. When the function ended, Vernon Maitland, who owned Excelsior Coaches in Bournemouth, invited all the British delegation of about 40 people to his room for a farewell party, but asked us to give him 15 minutes to get some drinks sent up.

We had a little bit left from our £80 so decided to go into the casino to pass the time while waiting. Patsy put in the coins and I pulled the handle of the one-arm bandit. "That's the last coin," she said and I pulled the handle. The machine went mad and all kinds of sounds started coming from it. Everyone turned to look in our direction. Patsy said, "What's happened?" I said, "We've won the jackpot." "How much is that? " She asked. I worked it out from dollars to pounds and it came to around £1500 – worth nearly £5,000 today.

Everybody was coming over to congratulate us and we were there a long time until a large casino official arrived and said, "You're English. You know you'll have to pay tax." He then took our passports and said he would be back. He came back later and said would I clear the machine. By this he meant put another coin in but neither me nor Patsy had any more coins. I said, "Iif you want it cleared you will have to lend me the money," which he did and at last the machine stopped belting out the noise that had been going on for almost half an hour. This is done on purpose to encourage others to gamble more. He then said, "You will not have to pay tax as we have an agreement with UK."

He took us to the cash desk and the female cashier counted out the money in $100 bills. As she finished, and before I could even pick up the money, the man demanded to be paid back his 25 cents!

Heart Attack

It was the last week in September 1986 when I had a heart attack while working in my office. Patsy took to me to our GP and he sent us straight to A & E with a letter. Two weeks later I had to go in for a battery of tests and then the last week in October 1986 had an appointment with Keith Ross to get my results. I knew him through business as he had been in my office ordering a 20-seater coach for a seminar he had in February, the same as he had the year before when about 14 people came from around the world to attend.

I went in and sat down to hear the verdict. He said, "You need a quadruple heart bypass." This was a very rare operation in those days. He also told me that there was a year's waiting list. I said, "Well I hope I live until February to look after your seminar again. He looked at me more closely and said, "Of course. You're Mr. Rowe from Summerfields." He then looked in his diary and said, "I can fit you in the first week in December". He must have been really keen to make sure his seminar took place on time.

That evening I was at home when the phone rang and it was Mr Ross again. He said, "I have made a big mistake I am in America teaching on the date I gave you." Then he asked would I be prepared to be in hospital over Christmas? You are not going to say "no" when it's your life at stake are you so I went in and they operated two days before Christmas Day.

He came to see me with his team the day before the operation and explained what would happen. He also explained that after I would wake up in intensive care with tubes coming out of me everywhere, and the sound of pounding in my ears - but not to worry. When I did come round it was because they shook me to see if I was OK as I had slept for two whole days. On Christmas day he came to see me and brought his daughter with him. She was training to be a doctor and when they had gone the sister came to see me and said, "You must be someone special because in all the years I have been here I have never seen him come in over Christmas." Later he became Sir Keith Ross.

On Boxing Day, Patsy came in to see me with our Lin, Dales' wife, and told me that Dale was in a ward below with a broken jaw. He had broken it going up to head a ball playing football in the morning. The next afternoon I asked sister if I could go down to the floor below to see my son but when I got there the ward was empty. In those days they used to put as many patients as possible into other wards over the Christmas period so staff could have time off. They had put our Dale in the children's ward at the other end of the hospital. When I got there I met a sister I knew because she was a customer of our video shop. She was on duty with two nurses. She told them I had come to visit my son and that I had just had a quadruple heart bypass. The sister told me "You will not recognize him," and showed me to his bed. His face was blown up and he had wires holding his jaw in place. When I left to return the sister said "You are not walking all that way back on your own." And called a porter to push me back in a wheelchair.

After I had been out of hospital a few days I noticed where they had taken a vein out of my leg from my ankle to the top of my leg and that it had become infected. So I went straight back to the ward and saw the sister. She said, "Mr Ross is on his rounds and I will get him to see you." He took one look at it and said, "Find a bed, sister." and I spent another five days in hospital.

It was three months later that I had another heart attack and after tests they found that three of the arteries had packed up. Good job it was not the main one otherwise I would not be here. My heart from then on has only been working at 70%. And they would not be able to give me a general anaesthetic again as my heart would be too weak to take it.

The Great Storm

1987 is a memorable year for most people over a certain age because of the great storm that struck Southern England in October. On that day I was going to a SKAL meeting in Glasgow and flying from Gatwick and gave a lift to a friend. Our plane was delayed because of the strong winds. We stood around in the departure lounge at Gatwick waiting to hear what would happen when an announcement came over the Tannoy asking us to move away from the windows. We moved away and a few minutes later they caved in under the pressure of the gale. Eventually we were allowed to board a plane but then sat for an hour on the runway until a gap came in the wind. The meeting started at 2 pm and we arrived at 4 pm. Then at 4:30 they said those going back to Gatwick must get to the airport as the last plane is leaving today.

On arrival at the airport we found the plane had been delayed again and were each given a £5 voucher to spend in a shop or restaurant but we had only just got in the shop when the call came to board the plane so we grabbed what we could and raced to get aboard. It was a rough flight and on the drive home from Gatwick there were diversions everywhere because of trees fallen across the roads. The journey took us an extra hour, but we arrived safely.

The same year as the big storm there was a SKAL International meeting in Sydney, Australia. Patsy and myself, Jack and Margaret and Brien and Paulette from Guernsey all took the opportunity to go on holiday to the Hamilton Islands. We flew by Ansett jet from Mainland Australia and the island we landed at was so small the airport runway went from one side of the island to the other.

We had a wonderful few days and when our time was up I went down to confirm our flight back to Cairns. It was a very small office in a big hanger with open ends and seats spread around the place. The lady I spoke to said, "I'm afraid the plane is fully booked but as you are SKAL members we have arranged a private plane for you." I went back to our apartment but did not tell them about the change. When the next day we arrived at the airport we met several Skalleagues who were also on holiday and going to the same place as us. A large plane came in and they all got up to walk out to it but I said to my group, "Sit down – that's not our plane." They wouldn't believe me at first and then I told them we had a private plane to ourselves. Shortly after, a small six-seater prop plane came in to land, we walked out, got on, and strapped in. The pilot was very relaxed. He said, "If you want a coffee pull out these drawers and you'll find it inside." He sat studying various maps and we were beginning to wonder if he knew where we were going and just how long it was going to take us to get back. Eventually we took off and landed back at Cairns, got to our hotel and went straight into the swimming pool. About half an hour later the other SKAL members arrived. The Ansett airplane had landed somewhere else to drop passengers before coming here, so our plane was faster in the end.

As the 1980s drew to a close the road accident gremlin that has followed me around for years was still dogging me. In 1988 I drove a coachload of medical students to Knowle hospital and after dropping them came back down Knowle Lane in the empty coach. That road has several bends in it and as I was approaching one a lorry which picks up skips came round the bend at a very fast speed. I knew he was going to hit me in a few seconds so put the coach hard against the hedge on my near side and slammed the brakes on so that I had almost stopped when the impact came. He hit the front near my driver's seat, bounced off and stopped about 25 yards past the coach. The windscreen was shattered and there was extensive damage to the front corner. I was lucky I was driving a German Setra which were constructed all of steel. If it had been an English made coach one like a Plaxton or Duple, which were mostly fibre glass, I would have been killed because he would have gone straight through me. So maybe luck was on my side after all.

The 1980s ended as they had begun with a SKAL international meeting. This time it was in Vancouver. As usual there was a banquet on the last night where Patsy and myself were sat with friends we knew from the Brighton club. As it was near Christmas we all got very merry. When the party was over, we were the last to leave and someone suggested we take the Christmas tree home with us. It stood in the corner and must have been 15 feet tall. So we pulled it down and got it through the door to the hallway but when we got to the main door the security chaps stopped us and said, "Where do you think you are going with that?" We explained that we were taking it home. The guard he replied "I don't think they will allow it on the plane." We looked at one another and burst out laughing when we realized what we were doing. That's drink for you!

Patsy and me when we first met.

Top: *Patsy and me get married, 1972.* ***Bottom:*** *We celebrate in Spain, 1972.*

Chapter 6
1990s – Our Roller Coaster Years

The 1990s were just as eventful as the previous decade. It started with a fire – and yet another accident.

In 1990 I was in Cardiff with Patsy at a coach symposium for three days with our friends Mike and Hazel. On the last day I had a SKAL meeting at a hotel at Heathrow Airport so I arranged with Mike to bring Patsy back home. I was sat in the hotel at Heathrow having a drink when our National President brought me a note from reception. As he handed it to me he said, "You may want to leave straight away." I looked at the note and it told me there had been a fire at the yard - two coaches had burned out and two others had been damaged. I knew there was nothing to be gained by rushing home instantly – the damage had been done. So I finished my meeting and went back after lunch.

This happened on a Monday and it appeared that two teenagers had run away from a home in Havant, had come to Southampton on Sunday, climbed over the wall and broke into a coach. They set the seat alight and of course it spread. The police arrested them and they appeared in court on the same day. To my amazement, they were ordered to be put in care at a home right near our yard where they had caused the fire. How stupid can magistrates get? Of course, that night we had screens smashed as they threw bricks over the wall. When I arrived at the yard it did not look as bad as I feared because the drivers had got together, hired a skip and shovelled the mess away. They had done a splendid job and the place looked spick and span.

On one side of Summerfield Coaches' yard was a row of trees which had grown very tall and were hanging over the yard's perimeter wall. I decided to cut them back and erected a platform on top of a 12 foot step ladder where I stood with a chain saw, cutting the branches back. I must have reached too high. The next thing I remember was falling backwards and landing on solid concrete. I must have knocked myself out for a few minutes and then one of my drivers, Lee, came back from our offices across the road, saw me lying there and took me to hospital. I had damaged my shoulder and had to go for physio for the next four weeks and I had severe bruising on my back. But it was not until about eight years later that I found out the full facts about the fall.

I was starting to have difficulty with my legs so the hospital gave me an MRI scan on the bottom of my spine and found I had multiple crushing of the nerves. There was nothing they could do about it not only because of my health but because, even if I had been fully fit they would not risk an operation because it could have paralysed me altogether. So I now have a dropped foot.

An Odd Timeshare

Later the same year, 1990, we went on holiday with Jack and Margaret to Phuket in Thailand. We both had time shares so exchanged them for one week's holiday. They were in separate locations but they had also booked a hotel for the first night and us for our last night as the dates of our time shares were one day difference.

On arriving at ours we walked into reception and found a lady sat with her feet on the counter doing some knitting. She seemed surprised to see us and ran to get the manager. Then another lady showed us to our place. It was on stilts on a hill and the decking on the outside had a hole in it big enough for someone to fall through. There were bare wires showing everywhere inside on the walls leading to the lamps and the whole place looked far from clean.

I asked where the swimming pool was and she showed us. It was thick with weed and smelt. There were also two great big frogs sitting in it - and when I say big, I mean the size of a small dog – both making a horrible croaking sound. We straight away phoned our friends to see if the hotel could take us in but they were fully booked that night so we were forced to stay at this Thai version of "Fawlty Towers".

We went down to the bar and I asked for two Bacardi and Cokes. Sorry no Bacardi. Two gin and tonics then? No gin. What have you got? Only beer as we have only just opened. We chose chicken and chips from a very short menu but when it came it was as bad as the rest of the place.

The next morning we came down to reception with our luggage and asked them to order a taxi. No he said, we will run you to the hotel. We arrived as our friends were having breakfast and we joined them before they left. We then spent the next seven days at this great hotel on the beach and met up together each day and had a great holiday.

Sadly, the memory of this wonderful holiday was ruined some years later when we read that a Tsunami had hit them and the hotel was completely washed away. So sad to happen to such nice people.

Window Dressing

Taking the relatives abroad can sometimes be embarrassing. I was driving a coach party to Holland in 1991 and had taken my mum and one of her friends, Ruby, to have a break. When we got to Amsterdam I said I would take the coach party down to the red light district where the attractive girls sit in the window. When we arrived, I told the group to stick together, follow me and avoid getting separated. We walked down the famous streets with their shops, sex clubs and girls on display. Suddenly I stopped and looked around and realised mum and her friend were missing. I retraced my steps and found them staring in one window at a lady waving like mad for them to move on. Mum turned to me and said, "What's that bed for in the room?" I didn't say it was so embarrassing. I just said, "Come on. We're holding up the rest of the party."

My Double

I had some of the bigger local firms among my clients for coaches and one day I had a meeting with a director of IBM about managing coaches for a conference they were having at the BIC in Bournemouth. After we'd concluded our business he said, "Do you know you have a double?" I was very surprised to hear this. "Have

I?" I said. "Yes", he told me, "at the Southampton FC football ground. There's a person just like you that picks up the balls when the footballers have finished their practice before the match starts."

I just shrugged and said, "They say we all have a double somewhere". I was not going to let on it was me that was still the "ball boy". That job kept me on an even keel and made me realize that I was no different or better than anyone else just because I had three businesses of my own.

SKAL National President

In 1993, I was elected SKAL national President of the UK and did 18 months at the helm until 1994. I attended president's nights all over the country and SKAL nationals at Brighton, and Newcastle, Northern Ireland. I was most pleased of all with the SKAL lunch I attended in Belfast because "Skalleagues" from the Republic of Ireland attended from the south for the first time in years because of the troubles. I was on the top table and they kept plying me with drinks to which I kept replying that I must make a move or I will miss my flight. They kept me there another two hours and it was one of the best days I had in SKAL, they were all so friendly to me. What I did not know was that the person I was sat next to was one of the directors of Ryanair – no wonder they kept saying don't worry about your flight as they had already booked me on a later one. During my time in SKAL, I have attended nine internationals in Israel, Peurta Rico, two in the USA, South Africa, Australia, Thailand, Sri Lanka, and Austria.

Patsy was a member of SKAL as well and she served a spell as President of our local Southampton club. Whenever she and I attended internationals, we always took a week or more extra as a holiday. In July 2017 I was made a life member of our club.

In the same year that I became national President we attended a meeting of the Oxford SKAL club Presidents' Night. When we arrived at the hotel we were given our room key and on entering found the room with couch, chairs and table but no bed and wondered where we were going to sleep. The we noticed in the corner a stairway which led to a bedroom and in this was a four-poster. After the function we invited about 20 members back for drinks and about 2 am when we had all had plenty to drink we put all the empty bottles and glasses on trays and left them outside bedroom doors down the corridor so it would not look too bad for us. After everybody had gone we went upstairs to bed and later I woke up wanting to go to the toilet. I got out of bed, forgot it was a four–poster and smacked straight into the post at the bottom of the bed and found myself on the floor. I suppose because I had had so much drink I did not hurt myself and we had a laugh about it the next day.

Bowling

It was three years after joining Atherley Bowling Club that I was made junior vice president, next year vice president, then finally president of the club in 1995. It was an office I held for one year. I had a great time visiting and playing against other clubs as well as going on the club tour. I liked the social side of club life and met so many friends. I was a member of the club for 22 years. I served on the committee for 16 years and ran the kitchen and restaurant for 18 months and employed the steward and stewardess, Chris and Rose who I interviewed with my wife and Nigel Long. My wife had left the club two years before me because she was finding the drive too much as we had moved to Hedge End 10 years earlier and I joined her at Hedge End Bowling Club so I could be near her as she had been diagnosed with Alzheimers.

In 1996, the SKAL International was held in Bangkok, Thailand. About every 20 years the king is brought upriver by longboats rowed by his men along with a flotilla of other canoes. We were privileged to have front row seats in the stand on the edge of the river. Everybody started cheering as his majesty came into sight in the distance and then the heavens opened as the monsoon hit us. They sent a motor boat to take the king off the canoe as the river was starting to get rough. Of course, they cancelled the event and we made our way back to the coaches. We had left the roof and all the windows open because of the heat and the coach was like a river inside. Getting back to the town centre and going into our hotel we were soaked to the skin. The staff could not understand why we were so wet as they had had no rain at all and were only three miles away from the river.

In 1997, we were in Texas with Jack and Margaret and some Skalleagues. This night we were attending a black tie event and were all standing around when a man we didn't know came in wearing a dinner suit and a cowboy hat and western boots. He told he barman that drinks were on him. He was the managing director, Texas, for American Airlines. After the event he asked if we four would like to come back to his house for a drink?

We were on one side of Houston and he lived on the other side. We all got into his Cadillac and I got into the front with his wife, said Hi and saw that under her feet on the floor was an empty champagne bottle. He said, "We drank that on the way over." After a few drinks at his house he said, "Do you want one for the road?" We thought he meant a last drink at his house but he literally meant a drink to have on the way back to our hotel. He drove us, glass in hand, and gave us a guided tour of Houston. How he could stand up, let alone drive, I do not know. We got back to our hotel at 4 am, had to be up at 6 am as we were flying home next day.

Disaster

Throughout the 1990s we did private hire, our own tours plus corporate work and contract hire as well as having two coaches done up in the livery of Anglia Holidays, who we worked for all the year round. Then at the end of the decade, in 1999, a disaster hit us. We had already put a deposit on a new coach for the following year when within three months we lost our prison contract at Winchester on which we had 3 to 5 vehicles a day. We were given no notice that a company had been awarded a contract by government to take over all the UK.

The general hospital who hired two or three vehicles every Tuesdsay and Thursday afternoon for students to go to other hospitals in Hampshire took teaching in house. IBM usually had one or two each day, both morning and afternoon but now stopped them because their numbers had dropped and used taxis instead. On top of this the schools were cutting back on day trips. The result of all these cutbacks was that we got into financial difficulties.

My health was poor as well, so we decided to get out of the business altogether and let my secretary/receptionist Tracey take it over. I more or less gave the company to her, which was a big mistake. I should have tried to save something from the coach fleet, building and yard but I more or less gave it to her as she had been with me about 17 years.

I had been expecting to get about £150,000 which would have been my pension, but I got so low because of declining business and poor heath I let her have it. The company kept going for another seven years and then she went into liquidation and lost everything that I and Patsy had worked so hard to build up over 24 years. A sad ending.

Top: *At a SKAL International meeting in Las Vegas, 1984, where Patsy and I won the jackpot.*

Below: *On our travels, again in 1984, with SKAL International.*

Top: Still on our international travels with SKAL in 1987.

Below: Two Presidents of Southampton SKAL – one past, one present. Patsy and me in 1990.

Chapter 7
2000s - Moving House

They say house moving causes a lot of stress and I can vouch for that with my own experience. When I retired, Patsy and I decided we could not afford to carry on paying all the overheads of our existing house. It was a lovely home in Basset, in the north of Southampton. Four bedrooms and en suite, dining room, lounge, utility room plus a conservatory. But the house was very expensive to run so we put it on the market.

We were looking for a bungalow and found one at Lowford, made an offer and the woman who owned it accepted. We then sold our house, but then the woman who owned the bungalow phoned us to say she had changed her mind and wanted to stay where she was. A friend of ours knew a lady who was selling her father's bungalow in Hedge End, so we went and saw her, and made an offer. Then she told us she had another couple coming round to see it and would let us know. I gave her my phone number and reminded her that we were cash buyers and that we had come directly to her, so there were no estate agents' fees to pay. But despite this, later we got a phone call to say she had let someone else have it.

We were in a right mess now. We were exchanging contracts the next day, the buyers wanted to move in 14 days later and we had nowhere to go. But we decided to go ahead. Our daughter Kim offered to put us up. We said, "It will only be for a couple of months." It turned out to be six months. We then had to get our goods stored but we were very lucky. A friend of ours, Alan, who lived opposite was manager of "Van Pack" an American company who moved people around the world. So he sent his men up and they packed it all into a container and didn't charge us a penny.

It was about four months later that I got a call from an estate agent who asked were we still interested in the bungalow we had seen at Hedge End? He told us that the woman who owned it had come into the office asking if he still had our phone number. He said "Yes, but it would mean you now have to go through the office and not direct." The other buyers could not get a mortgage and so their purchase had fallen through.

Our son Dale lived in the road at the back of the bungalow we were buying but we did not realise until we moved in that we were directly behind him. As we had quite a large garden we gave him 12 feet from ours and he put a fence up with a gate in so we could come and go. We did it all legally and the solicitor said, "How much are you going to charge him for the land?" I said "Nothing" but he told me to put down £1 to make the sale legal. That reminds me, Dale still owes me that £1!

We moved in 19 years ago and our twin grandchildren used to just open the gate and come through to see "pops" as they called me and Grandma. We never went over their house unless asked because we did not want to interfere as they had their own lives to live. But we had some lovely evenings in the summer when they called us over for a drink.

Ten-Pin Bowling

Marriage meant I took up some new sports, especially ten pin bowling at Bittern Bowl. It was Patsy who introduced me to this sport as she was already playing in the leagues. We had both watched green bowls many times and said we would take it up when we retired but we went to Portugal on holiday and the hotel we were staying at had a green on site and supplied woods and shoes so we had a go and liked it.

When we came back home we decided to try and join a club near us and joined Atherley because it was near our works. In 2000 we moved house to Hedge End and the travelling got too much for Patsy so she left and joined Hedge End Bowling Club and I followed three years later. In 2012 when Patsy got Alzheimer's she had to pack up and I gave up one year later to look after her but still kept my membership up. I am now back there but cannot bowl because of my own illness but I attend all the social events and go on their bowls tour each year. During my bowling career I have been privileged to be made president three times and have been on 24 tours with Atherley, Southampton and District, Hampshire Bowling Association, and Hampshire Indoor Bowling Association.

I have had some great times playing bowls. When we went to Inverness there was always a tray with glasses of Scotch at the end of the game. I have taken part in a number of sports but found bowls the most friendly and there was always a great atmosphere and I have made some great friends. In my younger years I missed a lot of matches in football because of my work and as I get older I wonder what my next sport will be. I expect cards and patience.

Patsy and I were coming home from Atherley Bowling Club with our friends Alex and Ann on evening in 2001 when I was pulled over by Police. The officer said, "Do you know you were doing 40 miles per hour in a 30 mph area?". I had to admit that I had not noticed. He said, "I will have to report you for it but before I write it up I will get you to blow in here," and he handed me a breathalyser. I had not been drinking, only Coca Cola although the others were merry so the breathalyser showed up nothing. He said, "That's OK," then he looked at me more closely and said, "Don't I know you?" I replied, "Well you may do as I own Summerfields Coaches." He said, "You would not like your drivers to know you had got caught speeding so you had better just move along." and he tore up the ticket he had been writing. What a very nice policeman, and what a lucky evening for me.

I have to say that Southampton police have always been courteous and considerate to me. One evening in 2010 I was driving down Burgess Road and was turning into Hill Lane when a police car pulled me over. "You're not wearing a seat belt." "I know - I am an invalid", and I showed him my badge. "You've still got to wear one." I told him I have an exception letter. He said, "Where is it?" I told him it was in my locker at the Atherley Bowling Club. If you would like to follow me down Hill Lane I will get it for you. He followed me all the way there but as I turned into the club he just carried straight on. I do not know what I would have done if he had come in because I did not have a letter. My lucky day - again.

I was next asked to be President of the Southampton and District Bowls Association in 2005, playing against different towns and associations and also going to Windsor Castle to play the staff. I also had my own tour to Weymouth where on one match they played a trick on me. Bryan Hooper and Jim Barlow changed my stickers while I was on the green up the other end, so when I bowled I had the wrong bias and the wood went the wrong way away from the jack and everybody laughed.

I was elected president of the Hampshire Bowling Clubs Past President Association which I did for the next two years. I was later asked to be Hampshire Bowling Club President but after talking it over with Patsy I decided to decline the offer as bowls can take over your whole life if you are not careful and we wanted to share our life together more.

An Odd Encounter

In 2007 Patsy and I were in the company of Jack and Margaret for a couple of days in Dublin and were having breakfast in the hotel when Jack decided to go down to the shop nearby to get a paper. When he got back he told us about a woman outside who was begging and who had no legs. He said, "I have given her £1 - you should do the same". I said OK and when we went out she was still sat there so I gave her £1. We went into a shop further down the road and when we came out we looked back up the road but the lady had gone. Then we noticed her in a telephone box standing up making a call. We had been had. I wondered how much she made in a day.

On SKAL duty again – this time in Guernsey, 1993

Two pictures from 1996

Chapter 8
2010s – Health Problems

It was in 2007 that I started getting severe headaches and went to my GP to get someone to look at me. He brought the local hospitals up on his computer and most of their waiting times were three months but Christchurch Hospital was only 10 days so I made an appointment there and was seen in eight days by Dr Becky Jupp. She also covered Bournemouth Hospital so I went there for tests and later to get the results. She seemed very concerned about me as I had been bleeding in the brain (first time I knew I had one). She said, " I have referred you to Professor Martin M.Brown at the London Hospital in Queens Square." It was after the excellent service I had on the South Coast that the NHS now let me down for the only time. I waited for 16 months for my appointment where they said they would have me in for test. As I had heard nothing my case was taken up by the Patient Forum at Southampton who then passed it on to Hampshire then to London.

A woman called to say the hospital would phone me within 24 hours which they did and said they were sorry but they had forgotten me and would I come in for three days between Christmas and New Year which I did. But it was not until May 2010 before I got the results and a letter to state that in future I would be looked after by the Moyamoya Clinic at the hospital.

Years went by and I did not worry because the headaches had gone back at the start of 2009 so I presumed the brain had mended itself. Then to my surprise I got a letter with an appointment for 31st August 2017 - six and a half *years* after my last visit to them. I phoned and told them not to waste my time or theirs and to cancel it. Then I got a copy of a letter sent to my GP to state I did not turn up for the appointment which made it look as though it was my fault.

But while my own health problems seemed to solve themselves, unfortunately, we were about to experience one of the worst health problems, and one that affects so many families today.

It was a sunny May day in 2014 that Patsy said to me one morning, "I'm going to Hazel and Mike's for a coffee morning," and off she went. She had known them for over 40 years and we had been to their house hundreds of times as they only lived five minutes away. I was reading the paper when suddenly the back door opened and Patsy put her head in. She had been gone about 15 minutes. I started to laugh and said, "Did you get the wrong day?" She looked me straight in the eye and said, "I have been all round Bottley and can't find their house anywhere." I said, "But they don't live in Bottley, they live in Lowford in the opposite direction."

She said, "Of course they do. If they ring don't tell them that I got lost, just say I've been delayed." And off she went again. I knew something was drastically wrong so I made an appointment with the doctor. Later that afternoon I said, "What are you cooking for dinner tonight?" She looked at me with a blank face and said, "I don't cook", and she never cooked another thing in her life.

We went to the doctor and then to the hospital for brain scans. Two weeks later we got the results. She had Alzheimer's. I had been told by people that it comes on gradually but however hard I tried to look back on the last year I could not think of anything I should have picked up on. It was just as if somebody had thrown a switch. One minute she was well and normal, the next she had this terrible disease.

The first year was not too bad but it gradually got worse and she stopped recognising people who came to see her. Then our son came in one day with our grandson and she looked at him and said, "Who are you?" "I'm your grandson, Harry," he replied. "And who is your father?" She said and our Stuart was standing by his side. So sad. For the next couple of years I used to make a snack up and take her for a car ride two or three times a week and we used to go up onto Portsdown Hill, where you can look over to Portsmouth and, on a clear day, onto the Isle of Wight.

During our lunch stop there she would say, "What's that over the other side of the water?" And I would tell her and she would ask the same question two or three times while we were sitting there. Another place we used to go was Lee-on-Solent and again it was "What is that over the other side of the water?" And repeated it several times. She used to like it there because I went to the Bluebird Café and bought two coffee ice creams which we both agreed were the best we had ever tasted.

I now had a carer each morning to get her up and wash her and, later on, one in the evening also to put her to bed as I was in poor health and could not manage her on my own. I also had once a week someone coming in for two hours so I could just get a break. All the carers were very good and the day ones who gave me a break took Patsy out. Chloe took her in her car to see her pony. Denise took her to a garden centre for coffee and when I came back one day I found Vicky had brought games for her to play. I could hear this laughing and giggling and when I came into the room found she was making things with Plasticine. It was the last time I saw her so happy. She was just like a young child. I did not have much savings and it was gradually going down and if she had lived much longer I would have had to cut out some of the care she was getting. I know the children would have helped but I did not like to ask. They have their own lives to live and they have their own families.

The Government do give you some help but not enough and it takes so long to get it. They send a woman round to see how bad they are first. The woman that came to us brought two eggs, gave them to Patsy and asked her to make scrambled eggs. Patsy looked at the eggs in her hands and did not know what to do with them. The woman said get a basin and put them in and she did just that but I had to get the basin for her and she had no idea what to do with it. I would like to say a big thank you to Kevin at Right At Home of Fareham who supplied the great carers and also for understanding the position I was getting in.

On the 9th September 2017, my grandson Craig and his wife Claire came round to see her with their son Mason and stayed nearly an hour. When they had gone I went back into the bedroom and held her hand and within five minutes she had passed away.

It is always a big shock, although I knew it would not be long because for the last four weeks she had hardly eaten. One day

I took her meal and sweet into her as I had done since her illness started and she looked at me and said, "I don't eat". The most she had in those last weeks was half a biscuit to chew on and I had to coax her to drink.

It is not just the patient the family should worry about it's also the person looking after them. It is not only the mental fatigue they are going through but it drains everything out of them. I could not even stand up in the shower: I had to use the invalid seat. It took me around six months to get my strength back.

It was a great funeral - if you can say that about a funeral, but I am sure you know what I mean. Patsy loved jiving and dancing, so we reflected that in the service. We had American Patrol by Glenn Miller as we went in. Listened to Gentle On My Mind by Dean Martin, who we had seen live in Las Vegas and who was her favourite artist. We then all sang Dancing Queen by ABBA and on the way out Unforgettable by Nat King Cole.

There were about 190 people in attendance to give her a grand send-off. I was just glad she was in her 80s when she got Alzheimer's and had a good life, so many people get it when they are still relatively young.

Everybody has their own way of dealing with the death of a partner especially if you have been together for a lot of years, or even a short time. I knew people who had never got rid of their partner's clothes or other things and it's been left up to the family to sort it all out after they died several years later. Others take a year, some months or several weeks before they do it. I was different. A week after the funeral I started clearing the bungalow not only of Patsy's clothes but tea and dinner sets, ornaments we had bought over the years, pictures on the walls, even down to saucepans and cutlery. I stripped everything and only kept what I would need. My place now looks like a bachelor's place.

I will never forget or stop loving Patsy. I have photos in every room of her and the family to remind me if I ever need it and I have memories of many wonderful times we had in the UK and round the world together.

I often wondered how my step-children would react if their mother went first, because you hear so many cases where they break away and do not want to know the step father or step mum. But I should have not worried for all have been remarkable to me.

Kim, who is the oldest, is my power of attorney and I see her once a week as well as chatting on the phone and go for a snack some weeks at her place. If I need anything she and her hubby Steve are there for me. Dale lives at the bottom of the garden and we put a gate in years ago to make it easier to come and go, yet we were never in one another's pockets. On Wednesday evenings he comes over with Lin and we open a bottle or two of wine and have a good chat. He cuts the lawn for me and they both help me out with different things when I need it. Stuart is the youngest and he comes in to see me either from work or during the day as he works about four times a week but every day he phones or texts to see if I want anything and that I am OK. And about once every two weeks I go over to his and Louise's for a snack at lunch time. All three children invite me to their family get-togethers. I have two special friends in Hazel and Mike who I go around with plus a lot more in Hedge End Bowling Club.

When I go out in the evening or day time and I am laughing and joking I sometimes feel a bit guilty as Patsy is not sharing it with me. But it is when you get back home and walk through the front door that the loneliness hits you. The place is empty and there's no-one to talk to or share things with. Even when Patsy was ill, I could talk away to her though she never answered but it was still company in a strange way.

Now if someone comes in the back door and I am in the lounge they hear me talking away they may think I have got company but it is only me talking to Pickles the cat. Pets can be a great comfort to you. I do not know how much longer I have got to live but I will try and live my life to the full as I am sure Patsy would have wanted that.

At the start of 2017 I found I could not get my breath, my heart would not seem to turn over, if you know what I mean, so I was sent for an MRI scan on my heart and had to see Peter Cowburn at the General Hospital in March. But four days before the appointment I collapsed and they thought I was dead. This had happened about every five years since my heart operation and each time they thought I had had it. I went in at 5.30 pm to see him and he said, "I'm not happy with your MRI." I said, "That's funny only I collapsed earlier in the week." He said, "Tthat's made up my mind, you are staying in hospital," and he phoned the ward and at 6 pm I was in a hospital bed. He then told me he had referred me to the Free London Hospital at Hampstead and I had a lump in my heart and it was one of three kinds. One, he said, you can forget but when we know which one of the other two it is, we can give you chemo down here to cure it.

Back on the ward a nurse said to me, "You're lucky. You're going down first in the morning - and the other patients are not going to be happy." But what she did not know and what you don't hear about, is that Dr Cowburn had phoned his staff and said he wanted them in at 6.30 am so it did not affect the other patients, whose operations he was starting as usual at 8 am.

A doctor came to my bed and said, "We have got to keep you alive until morning as we do not want to call someone in halfway through the night." Which was reassuring in a backhanded way. The next morning I went down and they fitted a pacemaker set at 40. In hindsight I think one should have been fitted years ago and then I might not have kept collapsing.

I am now off to the London Hospital and it's May 2017 and they put me up at the Premier Inn Hotel no more than about 500 yards away, for three nights to do tests each day. At the end I had to see a lovely Spanish lady Anna Martinez Navarro who was in charge and she said I have some bad news for you. You have got a very rare wild type of amyloidosis that only about 350 people in the world get diagnosed with in a year and she gave me a minimum up to November that year, 2017, or a maximum of 4 years. So, I said, "Well, when you have got to go you have to, we are all dying the moment we are born."

I'm glad in a way about the result as I do not now have to have chemo. I go up there for a check up every six months and stay one night at the Premier Inn. I know it's a lot cheaper there than putting me up in hospital. They send a car to pick me up from

Southampton and to take me back there and then a car from hotel to hospital then back home after tests.

The last time I saw Ana I said I could hit most of those patients outside with my stick. She asked me why. I said they look so glum and miserable - if you are going to die be happy. I said to my children don't worry I might still be here at 90 years because this lump in my heart could have been there a long time and only came to light when I had the MRI scan on my heart. In the summer of 2017 I collapsed again at home and my heart was down to 30. They first thought my pacemaker was not working but at A&E they checked it and found it was working OK and since then and with discussions with London have put the setting up from 40 to 60 so let's hope I have no more trouble.

I also had polymyalgia rheumatic in 2009 . I had cataracts removed from both eyes in 2012. Then had surgery on my forehead and left chest for skin cancer in December 2018. I now take 13 tablets a day to keep me alive but that's an improvement - at one time I was taking 18 a day. I have certainly got my money's worth out of the NHS and will praise all of them any time I can.

One other story I must tell you about. I had a heart attack at Newcastle in Northern Ireland at a SKAL conference of which I was national President so had a suite at hotel where I could entertain other dignitaries. On the table were a lot of bottles of spirits so when the medics came into the room they did not take me seriously to start with because they thought I had drunk too much. Then Patsy put them in the picture about my health. I was then taken to Newry Hospital and put on a ward with beds so close together the nurses had a job to get between them. But in the three days I was in there I had excellent service because they had the best doctors as they dealt with a lot of bad cases during the troubles. But one thing I will say - the hospital was so cold it needed bringing up to date or being rebuilt entirely.

Chapter 9
Today – Where Next?

Everybody at some time looks back over their life and wishes they had done things differently. On the whole I have had a very enjoyable and exciting life and , yes, there have been some bad times - but you get over them. I have been all over the world and seen things I never thought possible as I was growing up. Yes, I have regrets about the people I have hurt and the woman I treated badly.

One of the worst days for me was a Christmas day back in the 1960s. I was sat in my bedsit with no food and no TV and all by myself all day. I think it was the lowest point of my life. I could have gone to see my mum, I had not seen her for six months but was too ashamed to go and see her. I know she would have welcomed me with open arms and given me the love I was crying out for. She was very religious but always stood up for me and never put me down although she knew how bad I had been. When she was in hospital and I was holding her hand when she passed away I realized what a wonderful person she was and how much I loved her. The church was packed for her funeral but I was to be shocked and surprised later when I got a bill for the church, organist and flowers. Mum had been a member of the church for 69 years, had been a Life Boys leader, ran the Boys Brigade canteen did several years arranging the church flowers and had served on church committees and went to church every Sunday and when she got to ninety and could not get there by herself they came and picked her up each Sunday. And after all that they handed me a bill - and they call that religion.

The world is moving so fast you never seem to have time to do things but to all children I say look after your mums and dads. Make time for them. For if you do not you will regret it when it's too late as I did. When I got married to Patsy I promised myself I had to change and I did for most of the time. She was my rock and I knew I could not go on living the way I had.

It was hard at first looking after three step-children. A few years ago at a family gathering I looked at the three children and told them that my biggest mistake was that they were not my own, I loved them so much. Patsy was six years older than me but age means nothing when you love someone and we were together for 45 years.

I have got no time for people you read about or see on TV that state that they have never had a row or argument in 40 or 50 years of marriage. All I can say is that they are either liars or have led a very boring life.

It is the grandchildren that most parents worry about - in what sort of world are they going to grow up? But it could be so much different with a few changes to the laws. We want the UK to be a place that you want to live in and be proud of and safe.

To start you have to make sure about immigration. We have to have immigrants and I am all for it, otherwise our hospitals would grind to a halt and our businesses, factories and farms would suffer. But they have to be told when they arrive the laws. If they commit any crime such as murder, rape, fraud, burglary, GBH or are a paedophile, if found guilty they would automatically be deported if over the age of 16. But now some are put in prison, which we the taxpayer are paying for and are supposed to be deported after their term inside. Others cry human rights which I believe in but not in the form it is in by the European Courts at the moment. Some say they will be tortured or killed if they are returned or they have a wife and family here but if we got the law changed they would know if they committed a criminal offence they would be deported regardless and this would be a great deterrent and make us a safer place. Also any immigrant, if he has British citizenship, should have it revoked right away if committing any offence. The NHS is losing billions of pounds by non payments by people from abroad who use the service for treatment or operations and then go home without paying. This has got to change. They should employ a person at each hospital to deal with this problem as they come into A&E.

They should check their passport and details and where they live and phone numbers. I believe all people using the A & E should pay £10 or £20 either by cash or card. This would stop some people who just waste A&E time and should never go there in the first place.

All governments keep putting more cash into the NHS but it will never be enough because science is moving so fast and they can now do operations we never thought possible. Also immigrants coming into this country should be told they will have to pay to use the NHS until they have been here two years and have paid stamps or they have money and can pay a lump sump for the two years in advance.

The hospital must know the average cost of treatment and operations and this should be taken on a card and if there are difficulties and it costs more, at least you would have had the bulk of the money and the extra person employed would have made her wages back over and over not just in A&E. If they go straight into a ward she would have to go and get their details and payment and the money saved they would be able to spend on a better service.

The road fund license on cars, lorries, buses is so unfair. I do about 4,000 miles a year but you get a sales representative or coach driver doing 40,000 to 50,000 a year, yet to make it more even so that those who use the road most pay for it, all you have to do is add up the petrol, diesel and new electricity used each year for the last 3 years and take the highest figure for the UK and do the same with the road taxes collected and divide one into the other and the figure you get you add onto a gallon of fuel, this means that the person using the most fuel pays the most towards the road. A much fairer system. OK you are paying more at the pumps but you are not paying any road tax.

This would mean hundreds losing their jobs at the DVLA but other companies have closed and their employees eventually get another job. We often see people had up for driving with no insurance or road tax or license but a lot of this could be avoided. I have never been asked on any motor I have bought to show any insurance or license. If every time you bought a car new or second hand the dealer would have to check your insurance or license and the insurance must run for one year because you have got to inform the insurance company that you are changing cars and straight away they issue another policy which of course you will have to pay the difference on. So if your policy is six months old you would have to pay another six months extra and the car would have to be taxed for one year by the dealer and you claim back any months left on your old car. At least all cars would have first year insurance and tax.

The same with bikes with no insurance. Again when you buy a bicycle from a dealer new or second hand they would have to issue one year's insurance policy. At the moment if a cyclist hits your car or crashes into someone the person whose car receives the damage or the person injured needs treatment the only way they can get any money is by taking civil action against the person concerned and most people do not have the money to do that. It is like the millions spent on legal aid. This should not be given to immigrants and should be tightened up. And the money we pay out in foreign aid to other countries, for example India. They can send a rocket into space yet we help them for their poor plus where we give to countries where most of it goes into the pockets of the rulers. This has got to stop.

This is only a dream because the actions I have suggested above will never come into force because the MPs in government do not have the guts to bring in such drastic actions. They seem more concerned over their own selves and not what the public think

If all the measures I have suggested were put in force we would have a better and safer society for our children and grandchildren to grow up in the UK. I have always liked a challenge and from the age of 9 years it started and there have been many since.

A tip to get away with some of the things I have done – be quick thinking, always seem sincere. And have the audacity to say or do things – never show nerves or be scared. When going for a job, don't just sit there and listen to what the employer says, ask questions like how often do you get a pay rise, how many weeks holiday a year, do I get any training, is there a pension scheme and what chance of promotion, and make out you know more about the job than you really do. But if you go along this route and get the job make sure you learn quick otherwise they will catch you out.

If you have any idea for a business which you feel would be a success but you are worried about taking a chance don't be because in later life you will regret it. It may not work out and with any business it's a gamble, and if it folds and you lose thousands you would have learnt a lesson but on the other hand it could make you a fortune – you never know. But do not take on a partner – do it on your own. I know from experience of the past.

I was the only child but lucky for I had Mary my cousin who lives in Sussex and is like a sister to me and is two years older. As from the age of nine years we played together every school holiday so we more or less grew up together. I asked Mum one day why I did not have a brother or sister and she told me Dad would not allow her to have any more children.

A lot of people do not talk about death but you should. We all have to go sometime. So I have tried to make it as easy as I could for the children. I have made my will which everybody should make because otherwise it can cause so many arguments on your death. I have made a list of payments to be stopped or cancelled and a list of people to be contacted and a wish list for the three children for things they want from the home although I have given them most things. I have picked the songs for my service and done a speech. That leaves me just to thank a few people for making my life so enjoyable. First my family and my friends in SKAL and the coaching fraternity, especially my best friends Mike and Hazel Pressley plus their daughter, Paula, who has been a great help. A thank you must also go to Amy who started the book for me. To all of you God bless you and when I am gone think of me sometimes and all the good times and laughs we shared. I have lived my life to the full and more – plus I have done it my way.

A Postscript

Just before I go I will tell you what happened to me this year, in 2019. I was invited by Vicky to a concert at the Salvation Army Church in Hedge End where the family are members, as she thought it would give me an evening out. So I went along and have been to two more since. The first performance was a choir followed by an act by about a dozen autistic people, some of who could not speak.

Steve, with the help of Vicky and others, conducted the proceedings, and everyone followed whatever they did - putting their hands to their sides, or above their head and clapping, plus two sung a very short verse of a song and the laughs, smiles and happiness from them radiated around the room. This type of group was set up by Mencap and is now all over Britain as well as in Australia and the United States.

The next time it was a talent night and there were two young girls who sung solo and had exceptional talent plus four women playing two pianos at the same time, barn dancing and other acts. And on my third visit there was a mixed choir of which two families had three generations singing and the roof was raised by the sound of the Southampton Youth Brass Band.

I thoroughly enjoyed each evening and have to praise the officers and volunteers for all the hard work I saw them putting in to make sure that all of us had a wonderful time.

I used to attend church regularly up until I was 16 years old and had not been to a church service for 65 years so I was shocked and surprised that when I attended the 11 am service at what a difference time makes. It used to be that everybody went in their best clothes but now it is all casual wear and even jeans. We used to sing hymns with a lady playing the piano and now they have a live band. I enjoyed the whole service as it was conducted in such a relaxed atmosphere.

As I left they told me I would be welcome any Friday between 10 am and 1 pm – just drop in for a drink and a chat and make new friends or play games. I did not know the Salvation Army Church did so much. Would I go again? I think so. Perhaps not regularly but on the odd occasion.

I drove home, made a cup of tea and sat down in the armchair when suddenly my whole body went stiff and I could not speak but could hear things around me and see the cat moving. This was the third time this had happened this year and previously they rushed me into hospital, but this time there was no-one in the bungalow and I could not even move to press the alarm on my wrist for help.

And then something happened that I cannot explain. I had this peculiar feeling inside me as if someone was talking to me saying, You have just completed a full circle of your life and you are now back at the very start again. After a few minutes, life started coming back to my body and after 20 minutes I felt much better. You begin to think, is someone in the universe pulling the strings? At 16 I was smoking 20 plus cigarettes a day but in the last five years have cut down to 4 or 5. I have had so many accidents or collapses that I have lost count of how many times I have been to hospital and since the 1980s, several doctors have said they are surprised I am still here and very lucky to be alive. Yet I am still here. Why?

TRUSTED CARE AND SUPPORT IN YOUR OWN HOME

• Our care calls are never rushed (one-hour minimum up to full-time live-in care).

• We do not wear uniforms (a discreet service).

• All CareGivers are introduced to Clients in advance.

• We carefully match Clients to CareGivers with similar interests.

Quality Care in Your Home

Call us today for a
FREE care assessment
01329 233755

118

Outstanding* care and support from one-hour visits to 24-hour live-in care covering:

Southampton, Wickham, Fareham, Gosport, New Forest East and surrounding areas.

Our services include:

- Companionship
- Transportation and errands
- Meal preparation
- Light housekeeping
- Help with washing and dressing
- Personal care
- Medication reminders
- Post-operative support
- Holiday and respite cover
- Specialist dementia care

And much more...

*We have been rated Outstanding by the Care Quality Commission.

 **www.rightathomeuk.co.uk/solent**

solent@rightathomeuk.com

Printed in Poland
by Amazon Fulfillment
Poland Sp. z o.o., Wrocław